The God Who is *real*

Tested and proven through more than 55 years of real life experiences.

Richard Haverkamp

 FriesenPress

Suite 300 - 990 Fort St
Victoria, BC, V8V 3K2
Canada

www.friesenpress.com

Copyright © 2017 by Richard Haverkamp
First Edition — 2017

All rights reserved.

Unless otherwise indicated, scripture quotations are taken from the New King James Version®. Copyright © 1982 by Thomas Nelson, Inc. Used by permission. All rights reserved. Scripture quotations marked (KJV) are taken from the Holy Bible, King James Version, which is in the public domain. Scripture quotations marked (NIV) are taken from the Holy Bible, NEW INTERNATIONAL VERSION®. Copyright © 1973, 1978, 1984, 2011 by Biblica, Inc. All rights reserved worldwide. Used by permission. NEW INTERNATIONAL VERSION® and NIV® are registered trademarksof Biblica, Inc. Use of either trademark for the offering of goods or services requires the prior written consent of Biblica US, Inc.

No part of this publication may be reproduced in any form, or by any means, electronic or mechanical, including photocopying, recording, or any information browsing, storage, or retrieval system, without permission in writing from FriesenPress.

ISBN
978-1-5255-1189-9 (Hardcover)
978-1-5255-1190-5 (Paperback)
978-1-5255-1191-2 (eBook)

1. RELIGION, CHRISTIAN LIFE, INSPIRATIONAL

Distributed to the trade by The Ingram Book Company

"From the very first page, I knew this book would pull me in. Nothing prepares you for the true life experiences that Richard and Marina have faced in their life time. They have learned to lean on God in all circumstances and their faithfulness has seen lives changed, including their own. If you've got questions, the answers you are looking for may be right in front of your eyes."
–*Mrs. Susanne O'Connor. "Office Manager, The Spinal Garage Wellness Centre", Kitchener.*

"Rarely have I been so impacted by reading a book as I was at the conclusion of "The God Who is Real." Richard and Marina Haverkamp have served God for more than 55 years together, through "plenty and in want", joy and sorrow, constantly counting only on the Lord to provide for them, their family, and their ministry. If you are wondering if God is "really real", this very personal account will convince you that He is real indeed! This is certainly a very encouraging book for anyone desiring to serve the Lord."
–*Gerrit Blok, Co-founder and past Executive Director of New Life Prison Ministry*

"Although I was privileged to know about Richard and Marina's involvement in Belgium, I was unaware of the many interesting experiences during their years of missionary service. Their real life stories in this book are an affirmation that "God is real" and provides in many unusual situations. This book's easy-to-read style helps the reader to journey through the years with the Haverkamps and appreciate how God has used them to accomplish His work."
–*Mrs. Evelyn Hoffman. A friend.*

In a world often characterized by uncertainty, confusion, doubts, and distrust, it is such an encouragement to learn from people who have been 'on the other side', asking the questions honest skeptics ask about the relevance of God and the Bible. The majority of the time, we turn to biographies of people who lived and died a long time ago. But God has blessed countless numbers of us by allowing us to personally know the Haverkamps, and to now have the privilege of observing the adventure of their life as it is freshly retold. As I was reading the original version of this book in blogging format, I could barely wait for more! I felt like a child sitting on a rug in front of a fireplace, while Richard was masterfully recounting a story that not only drew me in but challenged me in my own degree of faith. This is a must-read for believer and skeptic alike. A true story of real people trusting a real God!

—Peter Bolton – Bible teacher, and retired Math/Science Educator (30 years in public high schools)

"In post-modern, post-Christian Europe, a most unlikely setting for seeing God's miraculous working, the author relates candidly yet engagingly, his first-hand experiences of the reality of God. As a friend of Richard, I can truly attest to what he writes since I have heard him tell story after story, not only proving the existence of God but how God stops at nothing and uses whatever method He needs to get our attention. You will love reading of a God who shows up and wastes no circumstance nor crisis to bring about the miracle of change that we need. What we all need is less theory and more reality, less orthodoxy and more life. The reader will not be disappointed as he reads about "The God Who is Real".

–Les Frey, for forty years active in Christian service in Spain.

The God Who is real. There are many gods in this world. In fact, everyone has a god. If it is not a heathen idol, then perhaps it may be money, fame, power, possessions, sex, or plain old self. In the end, every one of these disappoints. Richard and Marina have, through fifty-six years, discovered that there is a **God Who is real,** Who does not disappoint. They have tested and proven Him and they can unequivocally say, "*Yes, God is real indeed!*"

Introduction

I am a Christian, a true follower of a man who claimed to be the Son of God. Reading this may turn you off right away, but wait … are you honest, and do you have an open mind? Then read on. Here are 187 short stories about our experiences with God. You may say that these accounts are subjective—yes, you're right, but that doesn't make them worthless or meaningless, and millions upon millions of people all over the world have had the same experiences. They also have discovered that **God is really real.** This truth has come to them through two steps: first, they have read or heard parts of the Bible, and secondly, they have accepted Jesus Christ into their hearts. This has caused a radical change in their lives, which is amazing.

Let me take you on a journey to show you how God has become real in my life and in the lives of so many others. I challenge you to take this journey and see for yourself how really real God is. You will be touched and amazed.

My wife and I will be married fifty-five years in 2017, and we've known each other for fifty-six years. We have been serving God all those years. We haven't worked with an organization, since we felt called by God and have trusted Him to provide for us. God has faithfully met all our needs these many years—sometimes in amazing ways, as you will read. We'd like to share some of our experiences and answers to prayer, with the purpose of showing you that **God is really real!**

The greatest problem in the world isn't communism or capitalism, but egoism—the selfish human heart. The greatest need in the world is to change that heart ... but is that possible? Oh yes, just read on!

This book is about **God being real** and how that can change the world. As you read, watch for His **guidance**, His **provisions**, His **interventions**, and His ability to **change hearts and lives.**

This is a collection of short stories from real life. Most are in chronological order.

1. Birth, Immigration, and Disillusionment

As of July 2017, I have been a Christian, or rather a follower of Jesus, for fifty-seven years. I was born in the Netherlands with wooden shoes on and tulips coming out of my ears ☺. I experienced the Second World War as a scared little boy. When I was eighteen, I graduated from agricultural college and immigrated to Canada. Why did I do that? For one reason, I wanted to farm, and that wasn't possible in Holland, which is one of the most densely populated countries in the world. That's why I got to be so tall—one can't grow sideways, only upwards ☺! Secondly, I was looking for adventure. I wanted to be free and away from my parents, who were quite religious, so that I could do what I wanted. For two years I lived a bit of a wild life with a lot of drinking and all that goes with it. At first I worked on two farms in Harriston, Ontario, and then in house construction in Walkerton, Ontario. Eventually, I got fed up there and felt that my life was empty and useless. I made good money, though. I'd get paid on Friday night, and by Monday morning most of it was gone. Some of my friends had gotten married and had children, only to end up divorced and living unhappy lives. I wondered whether this was all that life had to offer, and I began to think about suicide. Looking back now, I realize that God was already at work in my heart, driving me to the edge so that I would seek and find Him. I also know from more than fifty years of experience that God is at work much more than we realize, working behind the scenes. Maybe God is working in your life too. Maybe He's trying to get your attention. Maybe He's driving you to the edge of despair so that you'll seek and find Him. Are there strange, unexplainable things happening in your life? Could it be Him?

1957. My last Christmas in the Netherlands.

2. I Laughed When Challenged to Read the Bible

One night I walked into a restaurant as the jukebox was playing, "What Am I Living for if Not for You?" Those words gripped my heart and haunted me day and night. *What am I living for?*

What am I living for? I went back to work on one of the farms in Harriston where I'd worked before. There I met a young man, a brother of my best friend, Martin. Martin and I didn't have much contact anymore, because his parents figured I was a bad influence on him. This young man told me to read the Bible. I laughed. Reading the Bible was for old grandmothers and little children. I had lived with my grandparents for a while when attending agricultural college in Holland, and my grandfather had the habit of reading a chapter out of the Bible every day after dinner, as was the custom in many Dutch homes. It was the most boring moment of the day! However, those words, "Read the Bible," kept resounding in my head. Finally, I looked for the little New Testament my mother had given me when I left Holland. Half the page was in Dutch, and the other half in English. I started reading and sure didn't understand much, but a funny thing happened—the more I read, the more I wanted to read. There's some mysterious power in that book! Not only did it seem to draw me to read it more and more, but it started doing something in my heart. A real struggle began!

3. An Inward Struggle

As I read more of His Word, I began to sense that God was after me, even though I wasn't sure there was a God. I'd never been in an evangelical church, and I didn't know anything about the real gospel, or the terms *saved* and *born again*. However, my inner sense that God wanted me grew stronger. I can't explain it, but deep inside I felt that I was to surrender to God and that if I did, He would call me to be a preacher. That really scared me. The only preachers I'd ever seen were a couple with dead-serious faces. They didn't laugh and they certainly didn't tell jokes ... two activities I really enjoy ☺! That was the picture I had of a preacher. I kept on reading and couldn't stop, due to what I believe now was the work of God's Spirit in answer to my mother's daily prayers for me. Much later I discovered that she'd had a real conversion experience at sixteen years of age. She never talked about it, though, as she had no assurance of faith—something that was never talked about in her church. I also didn't know that a few students at a Bible college in Saskatchewan were praying for me, one of whom was the young man who told me to read the Bible. They were praying for Martin and his "wild friend." One of the students praying was a young lady who would later become a VIP in my life!

4. The Miracle of Meeting the God Who Is Real

Back on the farm, I was really struggling ... or, should I say, there was a battle going on inside of me. That still, small voice continued to say, "Surrender." I realized that God wanted everything or nothing—none of this half and half business. He is the Creator and has a claim on my life. But my response was still, "No." And so it went, day in and day out, "yes, no, yes, no." When I went to bed at night, it was there. When I got up in the morning, it was there. Milking the cows—"yes, no." Out on the field—"yes, no." Why did I say no? Because I feared what would happen if I said yes. Later I discovered that many people are afraid of surrendering to God, because they think God will ask something terrible of them. Yet the Bible says that God has our good and wellbeing in mind. To be honest, I felt pretty miserable, so one day out in the field I finally surrendered and said, "Yes, God. If You are really there, You can have me and do with me whatever You want." Right there the miracle happened! The Bible calls it the new birth, which means new life, and I sure sensed that! Jesus said that without the new birth, we can't "see," and I found that to be true. All at once, I could see—not with my physical eyes, but with my inward eyes. God was there, and *He was so real!* How could I have been so blind? God says in His Word, "I will give you a new heart and put a new spirit in you; I will remove from you your heart of stone and give you a heart of flesh" (Ezekiel 36:26). Oh, how true that was! I had not shed a tear for several years. My heart had become so hard, but now I cried like a little baby. What a transformation! Could this really last?

5. The "New" Me

What a change! Incredible! I had indeed received a new heart, a new inside, and a new life. How real it was! All at once I could "see" God, "feel" God, "hear" God, "taste" God, and understand God. It was like getting a sixth sense ... much like being in a room that's filled with radio waves, but you can't hear the music and the voices. When you turn on your little radio, however, the music and the voices become audible. With our five senses, we can't receive those radio waves; we need something outside of ourselves to receive them and change them so that we can hear them. The same principle applies to God. We can't sense Him with our five physical senses; we need something outside of ourselves to reveal Him to us. We need His Spirit to come into us before we begin to sense Him. When people tell me that they don't see, feel, hear, smell, taste, or understand God, I tell them that they're proving what the Bible says about being spiritually dead. A dead person cannot see, hear, feel, smell, taste, or understand. I became alive when I surrendered to God, and what a change that made! It was *so* real! I was hungry in my new life, so I began to devour the Bible. I also wanted to talk about it. Some nights after work I'd drive up and down the highway looking for a hitchhiker so that I could talk to him about God and my new-found life. People around me began to notice the tremendous change in my lifestyle and wondered what had happened to this wild flying Dutchman. They saw the change on the outside, but I was much more aware of the change on the inside. But I still didn't know what had happened to me. Oh yes, I had met God and surrendered to Him, and He had come to live within me, but I was still quite ignorant about so much. It was only when I went to a Youth for Christ meeting that I found out what had really taken place!

6. Saved? From what?

The Youth for Christ event was the first evangelical meeting I ever attended, and I was thrilled. The singing and the atmosphere were wonderful; it all really touched me. At one point in the meeting, the leader stood up and asked for testimonies. I'd never heard that word before, as it isn't used in the barnyard and house construction ☺, so I bumped the fellow sitting beside me and asked him what a "testimony" was. He explained that people go up to the front and share what God means to them and has done in their lives.

"Can I go too," I asked him.

"Sure," he said.

I walked up front, a bit shaky, stood in front of the microphone, and told people that two weeks earlier, I'd given my life to God out in the field and that He had come into my heart, and I thought that this was just wonderful! That's all I could say, so I sat down. After the meeting, an elderly lady (and I mean elderly), skinny as can be and looking like she was already halfway in the grave, came up to me, pushed me onto a chair, put her bony finger on my chest, and said, "Richard, you are saved."

I looked at her in astonishment and asked, "Saved from what?"

She began to explain the gospel to me, telling me that I had sinned (as if I didn't know that already), and that, because of my sin, I was lost, but God had sent His Son, Jesus, to die for me on the cross and pay for my sin.

"Jesus also rose from the dead and has now come to live within you," she explained.

Wow! Talk about good news! I drove home that night in a daze, overwhelmed and at the same time overjoyed. **God is indeed really real.** What a new and different life I'd discovered! Yet there was something strange ... something I didn't understand ...

7. A New Understanding

I had now tasted fellowship with other Christians, so I started going to every meeting I could find—three times on Sunday and also during the week. I just couldn't get enough; I had such a spiritual hunger. But as I listened to the speakers, I heard again and again that we need to confess our sins and ask the Lord Jesus to come into our hearts. That's what bothered me. You see, I hadn't done that out in the field. I hadn't confessed my sin or asked Jesus to come into my heart. I'd just surrendered to God and told Him that I was finished with myself and that He could have me. Now I wondered whether I really was a Christian. At the same time, my experience of God's presence and the tremendous change in my life had been so real and radical that there was no other explanation than the three-letter word: GOD. Now, though, I understand it. You see, all sin, whether it be lying, stealing, adultery, or whatever, is rebellion against God. In Romans 5:10, Paul says that we are enemies of God; we are rebels, even though we may not see ourselves that way. What happened out in the farmer's field was *a rebel surrendering to God.* That's what conversion is all about! We've made ourselves God, because we do what we want to do. I, me, and myself—the holy trinity of man! I meet many people who say they are Christians, but they experience little of God. I believe this may be because there's a failure to surrender. Oh yes, they have accepted Jesus ... but they still run their own lives. Is this your experience? I was finished running my own life, and now I was about to find out what it meant to have God run my life. Exciting indeed! These were my first steps of faith and my first experience of a **God who is really real**, who answers prayer and provides!

8. Differences in Experiencing God

Before I begin to tell you about my exciting adventure with God, I have a word of warning. Sometimes when I tell my story, people come to me and say, "Richard, you make me wonder whether I really am a Christian, because I never had an experience like yours." Be careful! We don't all have the same experience. First, we are all different, so we experience God and spiritual things in different ways. Second, God deals with each one differently. Think of Saul (later called Paul) in Acts 9, and Lydia in Acts 16. Saul saw a light from heaven and heard Jesus speaking to him, while Lydia's experience is described as the Lord opening her heart. What a difference! Third, we all resist and surrender to God at different levels. Saul was fighting against Jesus, while Lydia was a quiet worshipper. I was resisting God, yet my wife accepted Jesus as a young girl in a quiet way. My experience was much more dramatic than my wife's, but she is just as saved as I am.

One of the main reasons I resisted God was because deep inside I "knew" that God would call me to preach if I surrendered to Him, and I was scared stiff of that. How did I know that He wanted that for me? I don't know ... I just "knew." So I said to the Lord, "Here I am. What's next?"

I got back in contact with my former friend, Martin, and with another young man, Henry, who had spent a year at a Bible college in Saskatchewan. We talked and prayed together, and we sent for our application forms. Would the college accept someone like me, who'd just become a Christian? And where would I get the money to go? I had none!

9. Preparing for an Exciting Future

I didn't wait for the application forms to arrive, because I knew I'd be accepted. The Lord would look after that, since He had called me! I started planning to leave for Bible college around the middle of September. Martin, Henry, and I would travel together in Henry's Volkswagen Beetle. I informed the farmer I was working for that I would be leaving; he was quite surprised to hear that his hired man was going to study to become a preacher! I think he thought it was a bit of a joke, because he smiled ☺!

Now I had to tackle the problem of where to get the money to go. I really had nothing except a bit of debt. I still had a few months to work, and I had an old car I could sell, but I wouldn't get much for it. I prayed and asked the Lord for help. I reminded Him that I was going because He called me, and I asked that He would provide for me in some way. The first thing He told me was to quit blowing money up in smoke. How did I know He was telling me that? I won't explain that now, but I will come back to it later. I smoked heavily, which cost quite a bit. I'd tried a number of times before to quit, but couldn't. Only people who are or have been addicted to something will understand me. I don't condemn anyone who smokes—that is a personal matter—but for me, it had to stop if I wanted the Lord to help me. I told the Lord that I wasn't able to quit, but I was willing. Could He help me? I was faced with the first test of my new-found faith. Would believing in God make a difference?

10. Experiencing Help from Above

I decided that I'd stop, but only after smoking for a few more days … and did I ever ☺! Then I threw the half pack that was left on the manure pile, never to touch a cigarette again. It was amazing how I experienced God's presence and power. At that point, I discovered that every time we take a step of obedience to God, He makes Himself more real to us and gives us new power. Believing in God made a tremendous difference. The experience I had may not mean much to you, but for me as a very young Christian, to be set free from something I'd not been able to conquer on my own was a real miracle, proving again that **God is really real.**

A second miracle also occurred. It was nothing big, but it set the tone for the rest of my life. Since the Lord had called me into His service, I felt that I should trust Him to meet my needs and that I should never ask anyone for money. I needed money and didn't have enough to cover all my costs, but I didn't tell anyone except the Lord about this. During this time, I was attending meetings, reading my Bible, and growing in spiritual things. Through these meetings, people got to know me and heard about my plans to go to Bible college. Several gave me a financial gift, even though they didn't know my financial situation at all; however, about one or two weeks before leaving, I was short by a certain amount. So what to do now? My prayer was, "Lord, are you there? Are you real? Can I trust you?" The answer came in an unexpected way!

11. Experiencing God's Provision

About one week before leaving, I went to a meeting. After the meeting, a lady came to me and gave me an envelope, saying that she was supposed to give it to me. I had no idea who she was, or whether the envelope had come from her or someone else. When I got into my car to go home, I opened the envelope and saw money in it—the exact amount I still needed! I almost fell over. How did she, or anyone, know what I still needed? It was absolutely amazing! Unbelievable!

If something like this happens once, you can say that it was just chance or luck. But when this happens again and again for more than fifty years, you come to the conclusion that God is there and ***He is very real indeed!***

In 1971, I took my wife and three daughters to Europe without a fixed salary or income. We had no idea where our money would come from. Our home church sent us support, which came to about 25 to 35 percent of what we needed, but we didn't know where the rest would come from. Some would say that it was very irresponsible of me to do that. Maybe it was, but don't forget that we'd already lived about ten years like that, and we had seen God provide again and again—not just with finances, but in many other ways. We knew He could be trusted! We have never asked anyone for money, even though we've had a few weak moments. We've always gone to the Lord, and He has met our needs (not our wants)! Now don't get me wrong—I don't judge others who may feel they need to solicit money, as it should be each one according to the faith God has given. But I am so glad I discovered that ***God is real indeed!*** More on this later.

12. Bible College an Adventure? You Must Be Kidding!

Not only did this experience boost my faith in a God who hears and answers prayer, but this provision also confirmed that I was on the right track. Now the great adventure of going to Bible college, studying God's Word, and then preaching it for over fifty years could start. Wow! In a way, it's sort of funny. One of the reasons I immigrated to Canada was for the adventure. Who would have ever thought that going to a Bible college could be part of an adventure ☺? At the same time, I was going with mixed feelings.

I knew this was God's calling, but I'd never enjoyed school and studying, so to start this again …? But now God was in it, and that made such a difference! I was on my way to discover the beauty and power of God's Word and the gospel of our Lord Jesus Christ. I didn't realize then how this would change my life and motivate and enthuse me to serve the living God and preach the wonderful and powerful message that has truly withstood the test of time. I preached it in Belgium and at conferences in twelve other European countries, as well as in Canada and the US. Again and again, I witnessed the life-transforming power of that message! Praise God!

Towards the latter part of September, Henry, Martin, and I took off in Henry's VW Beetle, which was loaded to the brim, and started on our way west, driving almost 3,000 kilometres to a very small town in the middle of the prairies in Saskatchewan. The college sat next to a farm, from which it was supplied with produce. One cold winter night, my roommate and I went to the barn and took a calf ... but that's for later.

I was overwhelmed with the vastness of the prairies and the province of Saskatchewan. I was born in The Netherlands, which can fit into Saskatchewan around fifteen and a half times. The population of The Netherlands is almost seventeen million people. Multiply that by 15.5, and you have 263,500 million people in Saskatchewan. But there are only a little over one million there, so you can imagine how much room there is ... enough for me to stretch my long legs!

13. A Calf in the Girl's Dorm

So here I was in a small town of about one hundred people, in the middle of the prairies, some sixty kilometres from the closest city, in a Bible college. Just in case some of you think that a place like that is dull and that students do nothing else besides studying the Bible and praying all day, let me tell you about some other things that went on there. Let's get back to the calf!

One day as we were sitting around the dining room table, the dean of women, who was at our table, spoke up and said, "It's been so quiet here the last while; nothing much is happening. When I was in Bible college some years ago, we had fun playing tricks and things like that." Well, she should have known better than to say that at a table where I was sitting. When I got back to my room, I told my roommate about this. Immediately we started thinking about what we could do. At night before going to sleep, we lay in bed talking and planning, until we finally came up with the idea of getting a calf out of the barn and putting it into the girls' dormitory. One cold winter night at about 1:00 a.m., we went to the barn and carried a calf to the girls' dorm, accessing it through the unlocked door of the furnace room. The building had several storeys, so we left the calf on the lowest floor and ran out after first setting off the fire alarm so that all the girls would wake up. We sat down outside on the steps of one of the staff member's houses and watched all the lights go on in the dorm. I don't think I ever laughed so hard in my life. The dean of women, the one who had been at our table, went down to the lowest floor where girls were standing watching the calf, and she somehow was able to get the calf up the short stairs to the main floor, into the entrance way, which was a small hall. She left it there, intending to phone someone the next morning to come and get the animal. What she didn't know, and what we didn't know either, was that the calf was sick and had diarrhea!

14. Enjoying, Confessing, and Punishment

The dean went back to bed, but after a while she thought she should check on the calf once more. When she opened the door of the entrance hall, she saw that the floor was covered with ... well, you know what, and it smelled terrible. She called the dean of men, Ron (now my brother-in-law), who got dressed and went to the bathroom, where he met my friend, Martin. Martin vehemently denied having anything to do with this, but instead said, "That's Richard's doing" and took Ron up to our room. Cleverly, we pretended we were sleeping and fooled him, so Martin and Ron went to the girl's dorm. While Martin took the calf back to the barn, Ron cleaned up the mess. The "wonderful" part was that my roommate and I were able to watch everything from our bedroom window, and did we ever laugh ☺!

A few days went by and no one had any idea who had done this, so finally we decided to go to the principal and tell him that we were the guilty ones, hoping that this would lessen our punishment. We went to his house and told him everything. He said to wait a bit and then disappeared. It took some time before he returned, and I noticed that his face was quite red. I wondered whether he wasn't feeling well. He told us we would have to clean the barn for a whole week as punishment. I didn't mind that at all; it had been worth it. Much later, after the principal and I had become good friends, he told me that when we'd told him the whole thing, he went to his bedroom, fell on the bed, and almost laughed himself sick. That's why his face had been so red. By the way, animal lovers, the calf got better within days. Whether it was because of being out in the cold or due to the pleasure of being in the girl's dorm (a privilege a calf doesn't get very often ☺), it had no ill effects. Several positive things came out of all this. Just keep on reading.

15. Apology

You may wonder how anything positive could come out of a crazy thing like putting a calf in the girl's dorm. Well, the first thing was very practical. Even though the school had fire escapes and fire extinguishers, it had never held a fire drill, strange as that may sound. But now, after some of the girls woke up from the fire alarm thinking it was somebody's alarm clock, it became clear that fire drills had to be held. Very good! The second thing is personal. Although most of the students and staff thought this had been a good prank and laughed about it, I noticed that there were others who were offended, so I decided to apologize in front of the whole school. The next day after lunch when announcements were made, I got up and asked if I could also make one. Permission was given, so I told everyone that the whole prank had been meant as a joke, but that I realized some had been offended, and I was sorry for this. You have no idea how difficult it was for me as a young Christian to get up in front of all students and staff members and apologize! I certainly didn't enjoy my lunch that day as I sat there with clammy hands, eating very little, but what a tremendous blessing that turned out to be in my spiritual life. The

Bible says that if we humble ourselves, the Lord will meet us, and He sure did. It was a very humbling experience, and it broke some of the old self in me, making room for more of the Holy Spirit. That doesn't mean that I encourage others to put calves in dorms ☺, but I do encourage everyone to humble themselves, and the Lord will meet them in a new way. By the way, only six months before this, I, a stubborn Dutchman, would never have gotten up to apologize. This again proves **that God is real** and able to change a selfish heart.

16. True Christianity: A Joyful and Singing Faith

Besides the introduction of fire drills, and the wonderful spiritual experience of humbling myself, there was something else that struck me at that time, and that was the response of the principal of the school. When he heard the story, he laughed himself almost sick. Why was that so special? Because here was a very spiritual and godly man with a real sense of humour. I was really impressed. Remember, one of the things that kept me from surrendering to God was the fear that becoming a Christian meant no more laughing and having fun. I understood how wrong I was as I discovered that Christians have lots to laugh about. Christianity is a joyful faith: the past is forgiven, the present is in God's hands, and the future is secure. Wow! I believe that God has a sense of humour. If you don't believe me, just look in the mirror ☺! Proverbs 17:22 tells us, "A merry heart does good, like medicine."

I also discovered that the Christian faith is a singing faith. The gospel of God's grace leads us to break out in psalms, hymns, and spiritual songs. Think of the thousands of hymns, songs, and other music, such as Handel's *Messiah*, written by Christians. Fanny Crosby, a blind woman, wrote 8,000 hymns. I was amazed when I discovered all this and realized that as a Christian I was rich indeed. Praise God!

When the noted agnostic Robert Ingersoll died, the printed funeral notices said, "There will be no singing." [1.] If you plan to attend the funeral of an infidel, agnostic, or skeptic, do not look for hymns or spiritual songs. Without God, without Christ, without redemption, and without hope, what do they have to sing about? At my funeral, there will be singing—victorious singing, praise God! I'm already looking forward to that ☺! Lord willing, there is lots more to come before that happens, because there was something else I discovered ... something quite serious.

17. Chastisement: A Dislocated Shoulder

I haven't told you much yet about Bible college. What word describes my life as a new Christian until now? Discovery! I discovered that **God is really real**, that He is to be trusted, that Christians can really laugh, and that we have a joyful and singing faith. The same goes for Bible college. I discovered one thing after another. It was just great! I was a young Christian and still quite playful. I've mentioned before that I didn't like studying, and after having been free on the farm, sitting in class every day for a number of hours and then doing homework and studying some more was a bit too much for me. Thank God there was a gym, and every night there were students playing volleyball. Because I'm quite tall, I loved that sport, so every night I was there. There was nothing wrong with that, except that we needed to do our homework first. Several students talked to me about that, as did one or two teachers, but I couldn't resist the urge to go and play in the evenings ... until one night when, I believe, the Lord stepped in. I was playing and jumped up to smash the ball over the net when at the same time a student behind me jumped up and bumped into my back. I fell over and landed on my right shoulder. I felt a terrible pain and soon discovered that my shoulder was dislocated. One of the staff members and a student drove me the sixty plus kilometres to the hospital in the city—an agonizing and painful drive. The outcome was no more volleyball and a lot more studying. I discovered something new again—the truth of the words of Hebrews 12:6, "Whom the Lord loves, He chastens." What a lesson to learn!

18. Enjoying Bible College, Preparing for the Future

You may be wondering whatever happened to that young lady in Bible college who had been praying for Martin and his wild friend (me)! Well, she graduated the year before I started at the college, and had gone to Holland, Michigan, USA, to study at the Child Evangelism Institute. I wouldn't meet her until my second year of college, so we'll just have to leave this most interesting subject for the moment.

The time at the college was just wonderful. I enjoyed the lessons, as it was all so new to me, and the whole atmosphere was something I'd never experienced before. It was so totally different, studying the Bible daily and having daily prayer meetings ... *so* different from working with a rough construction crew. Ever since my surrender to the Lord and new birth, I'd lived on cloud nine; it was almost too good to be true. God's presence was so real that many times I could hardly keep back my tears as I listened to the teachers expounding the tremendous truths of God's wonderful Word. The college had a three-year-course, but for those who hadn't finished high school, or who were older and had been away from studying for years, there was the possibility of dropping some subjects and doing it in four years. Because my English was far from King James proficient, and because I was having a hard time following the principal when he taught theology and used words such as "justification," "sanctification," "redemption," and "propitiation" (at times I wondered if he was speaking Chinese), it was decided that I would take the four-year course, which gave me time to also study English. But then, as I was enjoying the studies, the atmosphere, and the Lord, something happened ... something that really threw me off and made me decide to leave.

19. God Is Real? I Don't Feel Anything

The college had two three-day conferences a year: one in the fall and the other in April to close off the school year. Hundreds of people from the surrounding area and even from far away would attend, many of them staying overnight. These were times of tremendous blessing, with inspiring speakers and missionaries from all over the world telling about what the Lord was doing in other countries. I had been told about this conference and was looking forward to it with great anticipation.

Thursday evening came. The meeting started, the choir sang, the speakers preached, the missionaries told stories, and everyone was moved—except me! I've already told you that ever since giving my life to Christ, I'd been living on cloud nine. God's presence was so real, I could "feel" Him. But now, all at once, that was gone. I didn't feel anything; my heart was empty and cold. As the days went by and people were enjoying the meetings, I became more and more miserable. Many were often in tears as the choir sang and speakers and missionaries presented their messages. I had tears too, but not of joy. Mine were of frustration, as I didn't understand what was wrong with me. I went walking out on the prairies at night looking at the starry sky and asking God to give me a sign, to make a star fall, so that I would know He was still with me, but nothing happened. As the conference drew to a close, I came to the conclusion that I wasn't really a Christian. I couldn't be—others were so moved and overjoyed, and my heart was so cold and indifferent. On the Sunday night I went to the principal and told him that I'd be leaving the next day, as I was convinced that I wasn't a real Christian. He prayed with me, but nothing happened, so I went to bed.

20. Leaving or Staying? That was the Question

Monday morning came. You have no idea how utterly miserable I felt. I examined my heart again and again. What was wrong? What had I done wrong? Was there some sin in my life? I was so taken up with my feelings that I hadn't done any rational thinking, but then it dawned on me—I planned to leave, but where would I go? I didn't know anyone in this outstretched province. The nearest city was more than sixty kilometres away, and I had no money! So I went back to class and just sat there. For a few days I felt numb, but then slowly I became interested again in the studies. They started touching me again, and by the end of the week my feelings were slowly turning around, and I started experiencing the presence of the Lord again.

This was my first experience of what is sometimes called a "wilderness experience," or a "dry period." A Christian can suddenly lose the sense of the presence of the Lord, and he no longer "feels" God. The Bible doesn't speak to him, prayer seems like talking to a brick wall, and everything feels so unreal. Along with this, the person often wrestles with guilt feelings and frustration. These periods may last for a few days, weeks, or sometimes even longer. Why does this happen? There may be different reasons, but let me suggest just one. Once upon a time, there was a father and mother who had an eight-year-old daughter, Christine.

21. "Candies"

Every morning the father would go around the corner to catch the bus to work. Christine would take him to the bus stop and then run home to go to school. Every afternoon at five, Christine would meet her father at the bus stop. Her father always had some candies for her, but one morning he told her that he was out of candies and couldn't buy any where he worked, so he wouldn't have any for her later that day. That afternoon as the father sat on the bus, he wondered whether Christine would be there. The bus stopped, he got out, but no Christine. The father was quite disappointed and started to walk home. Suddenly, Christine came running around the corner and jumped into his arms. The father was overjoyed and realized that she loved him not because of the candies, but because he was her father.

I think there are times when the Lord takes away our "feelings" (candies). He wants to see whether we love Him because of those feelings, or because He is our Father. He already knows the answer, but He wants us to know it too and learn to live by faith, trusting Him whether we feel Him or not. That's what faith is all about. He is there, and He can be trusted. He longs to have us know that! What a lesson to learn! And now on to California, USA!

22. The "Tree"

Before we get to California, I have one more thing to share with you regarding my experience at the Bible college. When I arrived I met the different staff members, people who had been Christians for many years, and I thought they were all saints. I really looked up to them, until one day I discovered that one of the teachers had marriage problems. What a shock that was! Some time later I found out that another had problems with his children. Another shock! To make a long story short, I learned many had either one problem or another. Yes, they were saints in God's eyes, but they were still very human too. I learned a tremendous lesson, which was to keep my eyes on Jesus.

Some time later I remembered something said to me by the first farmer I worked for after coming from Holland. He'd put me on a big tractor with a large plow behind it and told me to plow a certain field. He explained that in Canada we plow straight furrows. He pointed to a tree on the other side of the field and said, "Don't take your eyes off the tree until you get to the other side." I started plowing, keeping my eyes on the tree, but in the middle of the very large field, I couldn't resist the urge to quickly look around. Sure enough, when I looked back there was one straight furrow. Pretty pleased with myself, I plowed to the other side, but when I got there and turned around, I saw that right at the place where I'd turned around mid-field there was a nice little curve. I believe that one reason we as Christians have curves and crooked things in our lives is because we take our eyes off the Tree—the Lord Jesus. So let's remember those words: *Don't take your eyes off the "Tree" until you get to the other side.* That's what faith is all about! Now, what about California?

23. From Choir to Camp to California

Allow me to repeat once more: *Don't take your eyes off the Tree.* Hebrews 12:2–3 says, "Looking unto Jesus [not people] ... for consider Him who endured such hostility from sinners against Himself, lest you become weary and discouraged in your souls." This is the remedy for discouragement: Consider Him! Keep your eyes on Him!

The end of my first year had come. We had a tremendous closing conference with the graduation of the third year students. Along with a large choir, the college also had a radio choir comprised of fourteen to sixteen students. Though I'm not a nightingale, I was part of that choir. Every Sunday night, the college would broadcast to southern Saskatchewan. The principal would speak and the choir would sing several songs. After the closing of the school year, the radio choir travelled for two weeks, visiting a different church every evening somewhere in Saskatchewan. It was a great time. After returning from this tour, I worked for a local farmer doing the seeding for him. How I loved that—driving the tractor and going around the enormous fields!

I helped at a children's camp in Alberta for two weeks in June, and there I met a man and his wife in their sixties from California, whose forefathers had come from Holland. They asked me to come and work on their farm; they had 30,000 turkeys and 400 fruit trees, mainly peaches and almonds. I would earn enough to go back to college. A few days later I flew to California, not knowing that there my surrender to God would be greatly tested!

24. Experiences in California

Eighty percent of the world's almonds come from California's Central Valley, an 323,749 hectares (800,000-acres) area of almond orchards. My employer, John Vis, had a farm where his son lived and where the buildings were with most of the turkeys. John himself lived in a small town, Denair, east of Turlock. He also owned orchards with fruit trees, mainly peaches and almonds. I lived in a large mobile home in the almond orchard, which also had several thousand turkeys in an enclosed area. The trees were irrigated from canals that carried water from the Sierra Nevada Mountains. One of my jobs was to move the irrigation pipes and sprinklers twice a day so that all the trees got watered. It was hard work, as it was very warm … often up to forty degrees Celsius or even more. Several times a day we would jump into the canal with our clothes on to cool off. Once the almonds were ready to be harvested, we would use clubs with thick rubber endings, climb a tree, stand in a fork, and hit the branches so that the almonds would fall to the ground. Then we would rake them together and put them in bags to be shipped out.

One day I was standing quite high up in a tree, lifting up my arms with the club ready to bring it down hard on some branches, when I felt my shoulder slip out. It had dislocated, which had happened twice before in Bible college. There I stood, unable to move. Another worker came with a piece of irrigation pipe and held it against my chest to keep me balanced, and I was able to slowly twist my shoulder back into place, which was very painful. I couldn't work for two weeks, as my arm was in a sling.

I became very good friends with John and his wife, and one day he made me an offer that made me reel!

25. An Unbelievably Tempting Offer

Every Sunday I'd go to church with them and then spend most of the day at their house, enjoying good meals and fellowship. I was still a young Christian, and they were much older and more experienced in the Lord. We talked and talked. They wanted to know about my family in Holland and the war years and why I had come to Canada by myself and so on. They told me about their family and background and experiences. It was just great. The work was hard, but I really enjoyed it. I also was very fond of the mobile home I stayed in, located right in the orchard with such quietness around me. I had such wonderful times reading my Bible and other good books.

During one of my visits with John and his wife, we got talking about the past again. I mentioned that when I was in my early teens, I had a real desire to become a doctor. The human body fascinates me (see the nine-video YouTube special *The Incredible Human Machine*), and I wanted to help sick people. However, this dream never materialized, as I knew my parents didn't have the finances for med school, and the Lord had other plans for me (which I wasn't aware of in my teens). Some time later while I was at John's home again, he turned to me and made me an unbelievable offer. He said that they had come to like me, and they wondered whether I would consider staying with them, living in the mobile home, and helping them as much as I could. In return, they would put me through university to become a doctor. I was twenty-one at the time, so that was still possible. They offered to pay all my expenses! I was flabbergasted and almost fell off my chair.

26. God's Calling: Doctor or Preacher?

What an offer! I didn't know what to say. I asked them to give me time to think and, especially, pray about it, which was fine with them. I thanked them for their love and generosity and told them that I was speechless. Night after night when the work was done, I would sit in my trailer reading my Bible and praying, reasoning with God about becoming a doctor, which I so much would like to do, and now the opportunity had presented itself in such a wonderful way. I told God that He can use doctors, and that I could become a missionary doctor, and so on. But as I prayed, the Lord impressed upon my heart that I was to go back to Bible college to become a preacher. Finally, after a long struggle, I submitted to Him, and a wonderful peace filled my heart. I told my friends, and they were very disappointed.

You may know the saying, "Man says, 'Give me tools and I'll do the job.' God says, 'Give me fools and I'll do the job.'" In the eyes of the world, I was a fool to refuse an offer and opportunity like that! Doctors have good salaries; I don't. Doctors usually live in big, fancy houses; I don't. Doctors usually drive nice, big, new cars; I don't. But I have something else—I have the inward joy of having obeyed the will of God. I have the joy of having been an instrument in the hands of God to change the lives of many, many people, and that, my dear friends, is worth more than all the things this world has to offer. I don't mind being a fool in the eyes of many. I have been called that, and I will continue to be that. I challenge you to become a fool for Christ. Become an instrument in His hands and experience His peace, power, and joy! A short time later I flew back to Canada, not knowing that while there I would have two special encounters.

27. Two Surprises

Even though my friends in California were disappointed, as true Christians they realized that I needed to heed the call of God. This did not change our friendship. In fact, two years later I would again work for them for about three to four months.

I arrived back at the college a few days before classes started. You might find this strange, but my first surprise encounter was with God Himself. He revealed Himself in a new way to me. For two or three days, I felt like I was in heaven. *The presence of the Lord was so real*, it felt like I could almost touch Him. This experience, one of the highest in my whole Christian life, is difficult to describe. I won't say any more about it, because some might think that they're not as good a Christian because they haven't had an experience like that. As I've said before, God deals with every person in a different way. At the same time, I discovered that the more I give of myself to the Lord, the more of Himself He gives to me. It had been a real struggle in California, but finally I gave myself afresh to God, wanting to do His will, and now He gave Himself afresh to me. Wonderful! *God is really real and really present*! Give yourself to Him totally and you'll find out for yourself.

The Fall Conference began, lasting from Thursday evening until Sunday evening, with many people in attendance. Missionaries from all over the world came and told their stories of God's work in the lives of people in different countries. At one meeting the principle introduced a young woman who was the director of child evangelism in southwest Saskatchewan. He called her the hardest working young woman in the province. After the meeting, I went to meet her at her display table. I had no idea how special she was, but I would soon find out, and both of us would be extremely surprised!

28. A Young Woman Named Marina

Let me just come back for a moment to my encounter and experience with God. As I said, the more of myself I gave to Him, the more of Himself He gave to me. The apostle James puts it another way: "Draw nigh unto God, and He will draw nigh unto you" (James 4:8, KJV). Do you do that? Do you really want to experience God? Then make time to draw nigh to Him by reading His Word, praying, and waiting on Him. But isn't that our problem today? We're so busy with everything else, we don't have time to draw nigh to Him. Isn't that what Jesus did by getting up early in the morning, or withdrawing from the crowd to draw nigh to the Father? Let's follow His example and see what happens. I challenge you!

Now let's get back to this young woman, the director of child evangelism in southern Saskatchewan. She would come to the college occasionally to teach students how to do children's work and run Bible clubs. I was very interested in this, so I attended some of her sessions. After one of these sessions, we got talking to each other, and she asked where I was from. I told her that Martin and I were from Ontario. She looked at me in amazement.

"You must be the wild friend I've been praying for all this time. What a discovery!"

Now I was amazed, because I had no idea that some students at the college had been praying for Martin and his wild friend, and now I was meeting one of them—unbelievable! Absolutely amazing. Her name was Marina, but more about her later. Suffice to say that she would come to the college to ask for students to go with her on evangelistic weekends in towns further north in areas where there were few evangelical Christians. One weekend the school sent me and a couple of others out with her.

29. What a Way to Start Dating

Allow me to go back for a moment to the introduction at the beginning of this book. I wrote "Richard and Marina have, through fifty-six years, discovered that there is a **God Who is real,** Who does not disappoint. They have tested and proven Him and they can unequivocally say, *"Yes, God is real indeed!"* Up till now, this book has been about me, and how the Lord touched and drew me to Himself, called me into His service, and led and provided for me to go to Bible college. But now the story changes, because another person, a wonderful lady named Marina, comes into the picture.

One Saturday, Marina, three students, plus a staff member drove about one hundred kilometres north of the college to a small town. We did home visitation in the afternoon, and two of the team members continued on in the evening. Marina had gone to a home where she'd held a Bible club in the past. Towards evening, another student and I went to that home too. One of the children of the family brought in a dozen or so young teenagers. They began playing records and dancing. Marina asked the father, who had been drinking, whether we could have a little meeting. He told the young people to be quiet and listen to this lady and her friends. Marina had brought an accordion along, and she and I sang a couple of duets; she sang soprano, and I sang tenor. We harmonized perfectly, even though this was the first time we'd ever sung together. I then told a story about a certain young man who'd left his home in Holland at age eighteen to start a new life in Canada. But he got into the wrong company, began to drink, and did other dumb things. Finally that young man got so sick of the way he was living that he gave his life to God and changed totally. I then asked whether they knew who this young man was. Of course, they had no idea!

30. First Time Evangelizing Together

You may find this strange, but I had given my testimony in such a way that they had no idea I was talking about myself, and they were very surprised and moved when I told them. When the meeting was finished, the father told the young people to follow our example and not his with his drinking habits. Most of the young people left, but a few stayed behind. We talked with them some more, and a couple of them accepted the Lord Jesus as their Saviour.

The team was able to stay overnight with people Marina knew. On Sunday, we went to another town where Marina had held a Bible club. We visited homes, inviting people to a meeting in another home. I led the meeting, and Marina played the accordion for the singing. Then the lady staff member told about her work as a missionary in Cuba. After that, I preached, and the Lord gave real liberty. I was amazed. We did some more visitation in the afternoon and then drove back to the college, very satisfied with the fruitful and blessed time we'd had. To me, it was a real confirmation of the Lord's calling into this kind of ministry. Of course, at that time I didn't know that over the next fifty years, I would be preaching hundreds of times in such home meetings, seeing many people come to know the Lord and lives being changed. What a thrill! I really discovered that the pure gospel of our Lord Jesus Christ is indeed the power of God to salvation, and is able to change lives.

Marina must have also been blessed, as I received a letter from her in which she wrote how thankful she was that I had come along and taken initiative in leading and speaking. She had done this herself in the past, but as a woman was uncomfortable in that role. About a month later, another small team of students went with Marina for a weekend, and I was one of them!

31. Ministry and Heart Matters

We drove to a town called Beechy and rented the local theatre for five dollars to hold a Christmas service. We then went visiting homes, inviting people. The students had a play, Marina used her accordion to accompany the singing of Christmas songs, she and I sang a duet, and I preached on the meaning of Christmas. We had bought boxes of oranges, apples, nuts, and candy for treats. It was a great service, and we were very blessed.

On Sunday afternoon, we drove to another town and invited people to an evening meeting. Afterwards, we were asked to come to a nurses' residence for coffee, but Marina felt that two women and a man wanted to talk. The driver of our car threw his keys at Marina and told her to go ahead and use the car to go visit them. I offered to go along to talk with the man. Before we went into the house, we prayed together in the car, as we usually did. I asked the Lord to use us to touch the hearts of these people, but I also asked that if there was anything between the two of us that should not be there, to please take it away. After I had received Marina's letter, I had written back and we had started corresponding. In between the two weekends, Marina had come to the college to teach about Bible clubs, and we had been together to talk about her work and also to practice singing duets. Slowly, something seemed to be growing, which is why I prayed the way I did. We went into the house and had a profitable conversation with the three people. As we drove back to pick up the other students, I asked Marina what was on her mind.

"I wonder whether the Lord is saying that we should be working together," she answered.

I grabbed the steering wheel and said, "Well, if I ever get a wife, I want someone who loves the Lord like you do." We drove back to the college with much on our minds.

32. Was This of God?

Right from the beginning, it clicked between us. No, it wasn't love at first sight, and neither did we fall in love. In fact, it took awhile before love entered into the picture. It ultimately did, and is now stronger than ever, but at first it was our love for the Lord and our desire to be on fire for Him that drew us together. We also shared a strong desire to evangelize and bring the wonderful story of Jesus to the people. We still have this passion, which is one reason why I'm writing this, hoping that some will be touched by the Holy Spirit.

Marina and I continued to correspond with each other and meet whenever she came to the college. More and more it seemed as though the Lord was drawing us together. It seemed to be the work of His Spirit to unite our hearts in our love and service for Him. At the same time, I was struggling as I had done in California when the tremendous offer of going to university to become a doctor was presented. And now once again something presented itself—a lady! I wondered whether this also was the work of the enemy to get me away from God's real purpose for me, which was to preach the wonderful gospel of Christ. Another battle was going on in my heart. What was I to do?

What I didn't know was that Marina was having that struggle too ... until I received a letter from her. Here is an excerpt: "I sense the seriousness of this, and I have cried out to the Lord like never before: 'Thy will be done. Oh God, help me to know Thy perfect will.'" We were both afraid to step outside the will of God, which was man's original sin in the garden of Eden. But how were we to know His will?

33. "Your Will Be Done"

The most important thing in life is the will of God. This world is in such a mess because people choose to do their own will. Heaven is perfect and harmonious because God's will is done there. Jesus taught, "Your will be done on earth as it is in heaven" (Matthew 6:10). My conversion was a surrender to the will of God; that's when real life and joy started. I had fought against God's will because I thought it was difficult, hard, and horrible, and that it would take all the fun and happiness out of life. How wrong I was! Romans 12:2 says that God's will is "good, acceptable, and perfect." How true that is! The happiest and most fulfilled person who ever lived on this planet was the Lord Jesus. He said, "For I have come down from heaven, not to do My own will, but the will of Him who sent Me" (John 6:38). Just before dying that most cruel death, He prayed, "Father, if it be possible, let this cup [of suffering] pass from Me; nevertheless, not as I will, but as You will" (Matthew 26:39). How could He do that? Hebrews 12:2 teaches that He did this, "... for the joy that was set before Him

..." He saw beyond the cross. He saw millions upon millions of people saved for all eternity; He saw you and me! So He did the will of God, the will of the Father. It's not always the easiest, but it is the best.

Even though I was still a young Christian, I instinctively felt that I needed to stay in the will of God. Marina had been a Christian since childhood, so she also knew how important this was. Neither of us wanted to do anything unless God showed us that this was His doing. We prayed earnestly and individually, but also when we were together, and then the Lord made it clear to us.

33b. Extra Edition. Did God Create Evil?

I wrote in story #33 that, "The most important thing in life is the will of God. This world is in such a mess because people choose to do their own will. Heaven is perfect and harmonious, because God's will is done there." I want to add something to this before continuing our story. This world is not only a mess, but it is evil—very evil. Oh, there are good things in the world, but look at the world in its totality. One would think that after thousands of years, we humans would have finally learned to live in peace with each other, but we are farther from peace than ever before. For the first time in the world's history, man has the capability to destroy the whole human race, whether through atomic, biological, or chemical warfare.

Many people struggle with all the evil in the world, and so do I. I get very upset when I see all the suffering, injustice, and corruption in this world. You may ask where this evil comes from. If God created everything, He must have created evil too. Just a moment ... What is the last thing you do at night before you leave the living room to go to your bedroom? You turn on the darkness, don't you? No, you don't—you turn off the light. Darkness is the absence of light. When we want a room dark, we shut out the light, perhaps by closing the curtains. Do you get it? This world is dark because we have shut out the Light ... God! Just as darkness is the absence of light, evil is the absence of good. And what or Who is good and the source of all good? God! When we shut or push God out, good disappears and evil appears. For example, in North America, God has been pushed out of the schools— no more Bible reading, no more prayer. And what has come in? Drugs, guns, teenage pregnancies, and other problems. In other words ... evil. What do we do to lighten up a dark room? We don't turn off the darkness—we let in the light. What do we need to do to make a dark world light? Let in the Light! What do we need to do to get rid of evil ... fight evil? No, let in the good, God. This is true for the world, for a nation, and for us individually. Let good in, let God in. Are you letting God in? Are you helping to let God into this world and thus change the world?

34. Seeking the Will of God

Many Christians find it difficult to know what God's will is for their lives or in a certain situation. We differentiate between the general will and the specific will of God. One example of the general will of God is found in 1Thessalonians 5:16–18: "Rejoice always, pray without ceasing, in everything give thanks; for this is the will of God in Christ Jesus for you." That's not so difficult to know, but to do this is something else. For many people, to know

God's specific will is much more difficult. Strangely enough, at that time it wasn't so difficult for us—not because we were better than others, but because in a way we had an advantage. Not only did both of us fear to step out of the will of the Lord, but neither of us had fallen in love yet. As mentioned before, it wasn't love that drew us together, but our passion for the Lord Jesus and the burning desire to tell His good news to as many as possible. All at once it dawned on me that this was totally different from what I had experienced in California. There the enemy tried to get me away from God's purpose, but now it was actually the opposite. Marina was not drawing me away, but encouraging and helping me in it, just as I was helping her. On a couple of these weekends, while others were visiting people, she and I had gone into a home and met with one or two families. While Marina taught the children in a bedroom, I held a Bible study with the adults in the living room, and God blessed that to the salvation of souls. We also held evangelistic meetings in living rooms, little realizing that this was exactly what we'd be doing in Belgium for thirty-eight years. More about discovering God's will later.

35. Marina's Background

Someone once said, "God's will is a series of God-given impressions that lead to a God-given conviction." This is a tremendously important statement, and we have often found this to be true. I will come back to this as we come to different crossroads in our lives, but before I go any further, let me introduce you to this most interesting lady, Marina.

Marina Funk was born on February 26 in Herbert, Saskatchewan, after a twenty-mile trip on a bobsled pulled by horses through the snow. Her parents were both Mennonites; her father was born in Canada, and her mother came with her parents and siblings from south Russia. They fled that country in 1925 after the Bolshevik Revolution. Her grandfather, J. Nickel, born in South Russia, served as a minister in the Mennonite church there. He pastored seven churches in Saskatchewan and often visited seven other churches farther away. As Marina's mother's name was Nickel. I'd tease her at times by saying that I married half a nickel. She'd laugh and say, "Well, at least I'm 2½ cents worth; you're not worth anything. Hah!"

Marina accepted the Lord Jesus as her Saviour at a young age. When she was six years old, her mother found her in the garden eating grass. When she was asked why she was doing that, she answered that she was preparing herself to be a missionary in Africa. From the age of twelve she dedicated her life to the Lord. Romans 12:1–2 was very special to her:

"I beseech you therefore, brethren, by the mercies of God, that you present your bodies a living sacrifice, holy, acceptable to God, which is your reasonable service. And do not be conformed to this world, but be transformed by the renewing of your mind, that you may prove what is that good and acceptable and perfect will of God."

Here's more now about this special lady whom I've known now for fifty-six years.

36. Seeking God's Will

A very young Marina heard the call of God to go abroad. At age fifteen, she travelled with her father, who organized Vacation Bible Schools in many towns and villages in Saskatchewan where there were few or no Christians. Some of her friends and siblings also went along. After finishing Bible college and then training at the Child Evangelism Institute in Muskegon, Michigan, USA, she became director of child evangelism in southwest Saskatchewan. She started children's Bible clubs in many towns and villages and taught others how to hold clubs. She also came to the college to teach the students and to get some to come with her on evangelism weekends. One weekend I went along, and that's where it all started some fifty-six years ago!

After that first weekend, I went along with Marina quite regularly and enjoyed it immensely. As mentioned before, we did not fall in love—we were drawn together by our passion for the Lord and His work. But as we worked together and experienced the Lord's blessing in the work, love also began to grow. Both of us were afraid to go that way, fearing it may not be in the will of God. We wrote a lot of letters to each other and talked whenever possible. We still have those letters, but we won't let you read them, as they are in a sense "sacred" to us. They give a good picture of what was going on in our hearts and how the Lord was leading us.

When discerning God's will, there were always three things we watched for: the inner voice of the Holy Spirit, God speaking to us through His Word, and circumstances. We found that when these three lined up, we had a pretty good idea of how the Lord was leading. And so it was now also: we experienced the inner voice of God becoming stronger and stronger, large parts of what we wrote in our letters were verses the Lord was giving us, and then there were some curious and interesting things happening!

37. "Love" Letters

Before talking about these things, let me tell you about what was going on in our hearts and show you just a little of what was in our letters. We hope and pray that some young people will read this and realize how important it is to have God first in their lives and in seeking a partner. Marina wrote me the following:

"Jesus is very close to me. He is closer than anything ever will be, closer than you will ever be."

"I love Him so much ... more than I love you, Richard, my dearest on earth."

"I'm so glad for our relationship, which began in the Spirit and is continuing in the Spirit and by God's grace will always be that way."

"Christ has blessed and enriched my life through you. Your letters are such a blessing and draw me closer to the Lord every time."

"I look forward to seeing you, the one who has added so much to my life. It is grace that brought us together, dear; it is grace all the way!"

Here are some things I wrote to her:

"Let us seek Jesus more and more and give Him first place."

"You mean much to me ... very much ... but Jesus means still more!"

"I long for you, but I long so much more to see God's will done in our lives."

"The Lord has been leading us thus far; there is just no doubt about that. How could we have such fellowship with Him and each other if we were not walking according to His will?"

We have been absolutely amazed at how God blesses when we give Him first place in our lives. It is really incredible. As mentioned previously, God's will is good, acceptable, and perfect (Romans 12:2). We have been so blessed over more than fifty-six years, that we have to pass this on to you and encourage you to seek Him and put Him first in everything, *for God is so real!*

38. Divine Guidance

I've always been a bit jittery when someone says "God told me." I think it would be better to say, "I think God told me," as it has to be tested by the three criteria I mentioned: the inner guidance of the Holy Spirit, the confirmation of God's Word, and circumstances. These can be very clear at times. For example, a lack of finances may indicate that God is closing a door. God's leading also comes in little ways; we call them "God's winks." For example, while Marina's mother knew nothing about us yet, she gave Marina a quilt for Christmas, which she usually only gave to those children who were getting married. Marina's grandmother gave her a towel, which she only used to give to the married ones. She didn't know anything either. At times, God leads in small details. After the close of the school year, we became engaged at the beginning of May. We hadn't set a date for a wedding at all, but offers came in anyway: a wedding dress, a wedding cake, a house free of charge as long as we fed some cattle every day. It was really amazing and almost overwhelming.

One of the college teachers told me that I was doing something irresponsible. How was I going to support my wife and possible future children? Marina and I had decided that if the Lord was calling us into His service, He would also provide for us. I was very discouraged after that talk and went to my room and fell on my knees, crying to God. It came as a flash to me: "Get up from your knees and read My Word." I got up and opened the Bible. It fell open to Isaiah 51:12, "I, *even* I, am He who comforts you. Who *are* you that you should be afraid of a man *who* will die..." What a fitting word from the Lord. That's all I needed! Talk about **God being real!** But be careful ... this is exceptional and not God's normal method of guidance.

And then the principal's wife talked to me!

39. Opposition and Blessing

When she and I met each other I greeted her, and she started talking to me, telling me that she had heard that I had wedding plans. I confirmed that, and she said, "But you signed the application papers in which it states that students are not to marry during college attendance. If they do, they must stay out of school for one year." I looked surprised, as I didn't remember that part of the application forms. I explained that we would just have to stay out of school for a year, as we were convinced that we were acting in the will of the Lord. She did not seem very pleased!

About a week later, I went to the principal and asked him whether he would marry us.

"I would be delighted to," he answered. I've often wondered what conversation went on between him and his wife! We set the date for September 15.

Between the end of the school year and the beginning of July, I worked on a farm and also sold Fuller Brush household products. I made enough money to get through the two summer months, and I was able to stay in my room at the college. During July and August, Marina's father, Marina, and I, plus a team of young people, held Vacation Bible Schools in eight different towns all over Saskatchewan. We went as far north as Lac La Ronge, more than 700 kilometres north of the Bible college. In that town, we had up to 125 children of all ages. Our schools would start on Monday morning at 9:00 a.m. and stop at 4:00 p.m. We'd run the school for five days, ending with a closing program on Friday night, to which all the children and their parents were invited. The children played a large part in these programs. Those were exciting and blessed times, but also very tiring. We would pack up on Saturday, drive to the next town, set things up, and start again on Monday morning. We came home at the end of August broke and worn out. It was two weeks before our wedding, and hardly anything was ready.

40. Divine Provision

We were convinced that it was God's will for us to be married. The prayer that we prayed continually was, "If Thy presence go not with me [us], carry us not up hence" (Exodus 33:15, KJV). We meant this with all our hearts. Before the decision was made, I spent another whole day fasting and praying in the hills close to Marina's parents' farm. I sought the Lord fervently, and once again received assurance that we were indeed in the centre of His will. And now we had two weeks to get everything ready. It was amazing to experience God's provision of large and small things.

We arrived home at Marina's parents' place to find some mail that contained financial gifts; one package was from my parents in Holland, who'd sent money for a new suit for me. Marina had a beautiful wedding dress given to her. An elderly Norwegian couple who had a farm and some cattle offered us their hired man's house, free of rent, if we would only feed their cattle twice a day. We also saw God's provision in smaller details. A lady friend baked a three-layer wedding cake, and one of Marina's aunts decorated it beautifully. When we went to pick up the cake to take it to Marina's aunt, we stopped in at a dear, godly friend's place. When we left her, she said that she felt a bit foolish, but she had something the Lord had told her to give us. Her daughter had just gotten married and had left some stuff at her place. She handed us a paper bag. When we looked in it, we found the little pillars that support the cake layers. We hadn't thought of those, and neither had anyone else, except the Lord. Amazing! **Yes, God is real.**

Next we drove to the print shop to pick up the 250 serviettes they had printed for the reception. We had no more money left to pay for them, and we never bought on credit. I still don't know why I went in, as I couldn't pay for them. I asked the young man behind the counter if the serviettes for Richard and Marina were ready. He looked around and said they were. I asked him how much they cost. He said he didn't know, and there was no bill with it. He told me that the boss would be back on Monday. All he had was Richard and Marina—no last name, address, or phone number, yet he let us go. Maybe what was printed on the serviettes was what made him trust us: "Richard and Marina, joined to serve the Lord. Psalm 121:8." I ran back to the car and told Marina that the Lord charged them for us. On Monday we went back and paid for them.

41. Marriage and God's Presence so Real

The next day, Saturday, September 15, was a beautiful, sunny day. We were married in a little church on the prairies in a very small town called Gouldtown. We had more than 175 guests, which was quite a number considering there was no one from my family present. The college principal preached on Isaiah 58:11a, "The Lord will guide you continually." Marina's sister sang from Ruth 1:16, "… wherever you go, I will go." And thus we were "joined together to serve the Lord," which we have been doing now for over fifty-five years. God has been faithful in providing for us for all those years.

The ladies of the church had a wonderful lunch prepared for all, and everyone enjoyed the wedding cake. We had no money for a honeymoon, so we stayed in a hotel the first night. Late Sunday night we drove to our small house on the farm. When we got there, the main house was dark, as the elderly Norwegian couple was already in bed. Our little house was locked, and we had no key! Because it was quite late, the couple must have thought that we were coming on Monday. So what to do? The door was like an apartment door, which opens from the outside with a key and on the inside with a knob. I noticed a window beside the door that opened by pushing it up. I figured it would be locked, but tried anyway. Sure enough, I was able to push it up. It wasn't very big, but it was large enough for my little wife to get through. So instead of carrying my bride across the doorstep, I pushed her through the window, after which she unlocked the door. We stood inside, laughing and rejoicing! What a way to start married life. Hah ☺! **God's humour,** *so real.*

September 15, 1962. Richard and Marina joined to serve the Lord.

42. A Miracle?

We spent six months in that cozy little house. During that time, we made trips to the places where we'd held Vacation Bible Schools to do follow-up. We also helped with a Sunday school in a nearby town, and I was the co-director of Youth for Christ in Swift Current. Most importantly, I studied a book entitled *The New Testament Order for Church and Missionary* by Alexander R. Hay. It caused me to study the New Testament in regards to the church and church planting, and it laid the groundwork for our later ministry in Belgium.

The Lord continued to provide for us in different ways. We had some interesting experiences. One day we drove Marina's sister to the home farm. She was on her way to a mission organization in Toronto, but she didn't have enough money for the train fare. We told the Lord that if anything was given to us that morning, we would give it to her. We stopped in at a friend's place in the city, and she gave us twenty dollars as a wedding gift, which we immediately passed on to our sister so she could buy her train ticket. We then started driving home. Halfway down the road, I suddenly noticed that our gas tank was almost empty. Has this ever happened to you? I whispered in Marina's ear, "We're almost out of gas. Pray!" We had no money at all, and we had given the twenty dollars to Marina's sister. How could God provide in the middle of nowhere? Without my realizing it, my hand went up and felt in the top pocket of my jacket. Lo and behold, I pulled out a five dollar bill. I have absolutely no idea where that bill came from ... I just know I never put it there. Are there angels? I believe so. Read Hebrews 1:14.

At the next lonely service station, we got gas and drove to the farm. We left Marina's sister there and drove to our home. When we arrived, we discovered that the Norwegian lady had made supper for us. As I lifted the cup and saucer from my plate, I found fifteen dollars. That evening, we went to visit the superintendent of the Sunday school in the small town close to us to plan some activities. As we left, he gave us an envelope with seventy dollars inside. We had given away a twenty dollar wedding present and had now received eighty-five dollars back. Is God faithful or not? He is no man's debtor! Praise His name. "Give, and it will be given to you" (Luke 6:38). *Yes, God is real.*

43. California: There and Back

During our stay in that little house on the farm, we reconnected with my friends in California. They asked us to come and work for them from March until the end of June, so we packed up and drove down to California, where we had a wonderful time pruning peach trees, and feeding and catching thousands of turkeys for market. We made enough money to get us through the summer and into Bible college for the third year. We spent July and August holding Vacation Bible schools in many places and saw wonderful things happening in the lives of children and young people. However, in one place, Piapot, we were at our wit's end by the end of the first day!

44. A Young Boy Experiencing That God Is Real

We had started on Monday morning with quite a good group of children, and it looked like it was going to be a great week ... but we didn't know David, a boy approximately nine years old. He was just impossible—interrupting all the time, running around while we were telling a story, pulling the girls' hair, fighting with the boys, and just being a terrible nuisance and spoiling it for everybody. That evening after the children had gone home, we called the workers together and held a special prayer meeting. We asked the Lord to either touch David's heart or keep him away from the school. The next morning there he was, bright and early. He came up to me and said: "Teacher, you know what? Last night in bed I asked Jesus to come into my heart." I almost fell over. I just looked at him and wondered whether he was trying to fool me. Amazingly, David had totally changed! He was quiet in class, he treated the other children really well, he was polite and eager to learn, and he told the other children to give their hearts to Jesus. It was just incredible!

David went on that way all week. A miracle had taken place, and we thanked the Lord. I had experienced that same miracle when I was more than twenty years old, but to see it in a young boy like this was really special. And it wasn't just David! During the two summer months, we saw many children become children of God. We realized that children can be easily influenced, so we were always careful to explain what it really meant to allow the Lord Jesus into their hearts, because we wanted it to be real. Many hearts and lives were touched, and what a time we will have in heaven meeting all these precious ones. What a privilege to be used by God to change hearts and lives for now and eternity. The beginning of September we drove to the Bible college, where a wonderful thing would happen.

45. Babies, God's Speciality!

It had been another busy summer, but we had experienced so much joy and blessing that it had been worth it all. However, we were glad to get settled in at the college, where Marina got a job working in the kitchen to help pay for schooling and expenses. Until school started, I was able to work for a local farmer doing some harvesting. Soon the time of studying started again, and how I enjoyed the classes and the fellowship! I often sat with tears in my eyes as I drank in the rich teaching and the beauty of God's Word. Some weekends Marina and I would drive "up North" to the areas where we'd held Vacation Bible Schools and meetings. We'd do follow-up with the children and visit the parents.

The time seemed to fly by, and then on March 23, the wonderful thing happened—our first baby was born. We had a beautiful girl whom we named Rosalinda, but for the longest time called Sunshine, as she was so true to that name. To us, every baby is a miracle, a bundle of joy, and evidence of the Creator. How happy we were! That spring when school finished, we moved to a small town in southern Saskatchewan and pastored a little church while also holding clubs and DVBS's in different places. Our little Rosa went along everywhere. She would sit quietly in class while Marina taught, never fussing or disturbing the lessons. In between classes, Marina would nurse her, and on we went … wonderful! The Lord provided in different ways; we were often amazed and so thankful for His care for us.

September came, heralding my last year of college. We didn't live on campus, but in a one-room apartment in Swift Current, a city about sixty kilometres northwest of the college. I drove to and from school every day, and in between sold Fuller-Brush household products in the city. Marina worked for some women cleaning houses. After graduating, Marina and I both had a Bible college diploma, and we were ready to serve the Lord … but where?

46. God's Miraculous Provision in Answer to Prayer

During college days, students would often get in contact with mission organizations. After graduating, they would then join a mission, do a year of deputation work to get the support they needed, and then go to a mission field. Marina and I had contact with a couple of missions, but we had no freedom to join. We moved into an apartment belonging to friends, and off I went to work on a farm. Before we did this, four young men from the college who had formed a quartet and sang beautifully went with me on a tour through Saskatchewan. At night, we would hold meetings in churches or halls, where they would sing and I preach. During the day, we planned to work for farmers to make some money.

But the day before we left, I still didn't have enough money to leave with my wife and baby or to cover the first costs of the tour. That night I prayed far into the night, reading God's Word and pleading with Him to provide. I was at my wit's end, as we would not be able to go if we didn't have the money. While reading, I came to the words of Psalm 50:15: "Call upon Me in the day of trouble; I will deliver you, and you shall glorify Me." I told the Lord I was in trouble and reminded Him of this promise. Again and again I prayed, until sometime during the night I received the assurance that He had heard me. The next morning, the telephone rang and a far-away friend asked whether I had received his letter. I said "no." He explained that a few days earlier, the Lord had laid it on his heart to send me a cheque, and it should be arriving soon. Sure enough, the mailman had the letter with him that morning. The cheque covered exactly what we needed. Although the donor didn't know about our travel plans and our need, God had heard and answered! *Is He not real?* I write this because the Psalm says, "You shall glorify Me." And so we left knowing that God was in this with us!

47. Missions and Provisions

After six wonderful weeks of seeing God work in many hearts and lives, I went to work on the farm. Marina and I continued with meetings, children's clubs, and DVBS's in different areas. After the summer, Marina had to slow down, as something wonderful was coming. On the evening of October 25, while holding a prayer meeting in our home, Marina suddenly said, "Richard, it's time." I got her into the car and drove to the hospital, where some hours later our second little girl, Lily Ann Joy, was born. What a joy she was!

Shortly after the birth, we moved to Regina. Missions was still much on our hearts, and we were seeking the Lord's will and guidance. During our time in Regina, I held special meetings in some places and preached in a pastor-less church for several months. We also got in contact with the New Testament Missionary Union, a mission organization working mainly in South America and Spain. It had an office in Fonthill, Ontario, close to Niagara

Falls. In May 1966, we drove to Ontario and moved into a small house owned by the mission. We fellowshipped and ministered in a small church nearby. Because of severe back problems, I couldn't work for a while, so we were trusting the Lord to meet our needs. Some time later, I got a job with Simpson Sears, but before that, I spent a lot of time in study and prayer with the mission's representative. One night before going to bed, Marina and I prayed together and asked the Lord to meet our needs; our cupboards were empty, and there was nothing for breakfast. The next morning after getting up I wanted to go outside, but I had a hard time opening the door. I pushed harder and heard something fall. Then I saw a very large grocery bag on the ground, filled to the brim with groceries. To this day we have no idea who put that there, as no one knew of our need, except **God—who is very real indeed!** We had a wonderful breakfast!

48. Called a Fool

Once my back was better, I found a job helping to set up a new, large Simpson Sears store. I was then asked to stay on and work in the men's department, where things like shirts, socks, and ties were sold. I worked there until June, 1967, and enjoyed it very much. One day the personnel manager asked me to come to his office. He expressed his satisfaction with my work and then offered to train me to become a department manager. It was a terrific offer. He asked me what I thought. I thanked him for the offer, and then said that I was sorry, but I couldn't accept. He looked very surprised and wanted to know why. I told him that I was going to be a missionary. Oh boy, that didn't sit right! Did I ever get it. He told me I was a fool to throw away a life chance just to go and tell people about Jesus. Most people didn't want to hear, anyway. He became very upset and told me that I was a big fool. I'd heard this before. You may remember that people in California offered to put me through university to become a doctor. I refused that too and was looked upon as a fool (see stories #25 and #26). The amazing thing is that God uses fools! Ha! I stopped working in June when my parents arrived from Holland. We hadn't seen or talked to each other for nine years. Transatlantic phone calls didn't exist back then, at least not in the places where I lived. What a reunion that was at the Toronto airport! They had never met Marina and our two little girls. After a few days, we all packed into our old Buick and started on our trip West. All the while, Marina and I were constantly seeking the Lord as to our future missionary ministry.

49. Getting Ready for Another Miracle

It was so good to have my parents with us, as they had just been through a very difficult time. I had two younger twin sisters; one died at age twenty and was buried on my birthday, May 18. A little over a month later, my parents came to Canada after having to say goodbye to my father's mother, who was seriously ill. She died while my parents were in Canada. It was very hard on them, but it helped to be with us. We took them all the way to the Rocky Mountains in Alberta and followed the most beautiful highway in Canada from Banff to Jasper through the awesome mountains, much of the time singing "How Great Thou Art!" We then drove back to Saskatchewan to be with Marina's parents. After driving more than 6,000 kilometres, my parents flew back to Holland from Regina.

After saying goodbye to my parents, we drove to the border of Alberta. A friend had a 12,355 hectares (5,000 acres) farm there and had asked me to come and help him harvest. On Sundays, I preached in a church that was without a pastor. I didn't know at the time that my friend was hoping to have us stay with him.

On October 26, our third little girl was born—Rieneke Ruth Hope. Rieneke (Renee in English) was the name of my sister who died. What a cute little bundle of hope she was! After the birth, the doctor told Marina that there was something seriously wrong inside of her and that she needed an operation. She was sent home to get rested up and then to come back for the operation. Due to our moving around through difference provinces, our Ontario hospitalization wouldn't cover the cost. What to do? We didn't have the money, but we did have the Lord and, unknown to us then, another miracle was in the making!

50. A Medical Miracle; Yes, God Is Real

We earnestly prayed and asked the Lord to somehow intervene. My farmer friend's wife had been a head nurse in a hospital and gave Marina some advice. Eventually, I took her back to the doctor in the hospital, who examined her and then asked why she had come to him. He smiled and said that he was very surprised. Everything was fine, and no operation was needed. When we got home and told the former nurse what had happened, she could hardly believe it. She said that she'd never heard of anything like it. Praise the Lord, He had heard and answered our prayer! All praise to Him!

Some time after that, my friend began to press us to stay with him, as he really needed me on the farm. However, we had continued to seek the Lord and felt that we needed to go back to the mission in Ontario. He was quite upset with us, but we knew we had to follow the Lord's leading. On Sunday, December 24—the day before Christmas—after cleaning the house and preaching my last message at the church, we left to drive to Marina's parents, arriving there on Christmas Eve. Leaving my "friends" place wasn't very nice; this was now the third time someone tried to hold us back from doing God's will.

We stayed with Marina's parents until after the New Year and then left to drive to Ontario. The first day we drove to Winnipeg, Manitoba—about 800 kilometres. Two little girls on the back seat, and Renee, the two month old baby, on a pile of diapers in a banana box between us. Every now and then Marina would nurse her while we kept on driving. The second day we drove to Sault St. Marie in Ontario—approximately 1,300 kilometres. It snowed all the way, at times quite heavily, but we knew we were moving in God's will and His protection. Late at night as we were getting closer to the Sault, the alternator gave up the ghost, the battery started dying and our lights slowly became dimmer and dimmer!

51. More Divine Guidance

We were able to drive into the city, thanks to the street lights. By the time we got to a motel, our battery had died completely and we had no car lights at all. We quickly went to bed, dead-tired from the long drive and wondering how we would get the car started the next morning. I got up quite early and, after prayer, got into the car. As I turned the key in the ignition, the motor turned over just once and then started. Unbelievable! I thanked the Lord and then drove to a garage, where they put in a new alternator and charged the battery enough to get us on our way. We left right away and drove the last 900 kilometres without any problems, arriving late at night at the little mission house where we'd stayed before.

While there, we ministered in the small mission church, did a lot of reading and studying, and had many discussions with the mission's representative about missions and church planting. I learned a lot from him, as the mission had been very active and successful in starting new churches in Mexico and some South American countries. At the same time, Marina and I began to feel an inner uneasiness about working with this mission organization. There were a few things we didn't agree with, but that wasn't really it. It was something else, which at the time we didn't understand, but which would become clear later on. One evening as we were reading the Bible together, a verse stood out to both of us: "You have dwelt long enough at this mountain. Turn and take your journey ..." (Deuteronomy 1:6b–7a). The next morning, the mission's representative came to us and apologetically said that we could no longer stay in the house, as a missionary couple from South America was coming back and needed the place. There were the three guideposts again: the inner voice of the Spirit, the Word of God, and the circumstances. We both knew very well where the Lord wanted us, but the time hadn't yet come and the details weren't clear. However, in spite of not knowing, we had no choice but to pack up and go.

52. Marina's Calling and God's Amazing Ways

But where were to go? We had been in contact with friends from Harriston, the area where I became a Christian. The farmer and his wife whom I'd worked for had both died, and his brothers were now working the land, but the house was not being used. I talked to them, and they told us that we could use the house rent-free, which we saw as a real provision from the Lord. I did some work for them, and I also did some other odd jobs, like house painting, to support our little family. We knew where the Lord wanted us, but we were still waiting for clear guidance as to the details.

While in Bible college, I had a very strong impression. The words came to me in a flash and really hit me: "The time will come that you will have Bible studies in the homes of people all over the country." I assumed that that country would be The Netherlands, as I had been quite burdened for my home country. Marina had a similar experience while attending the Child Evangelism Institute in Holland, Michigan, USA. I'll let her tell it in her own words: "One day a child evangelism missionary who worked in Belgium spoke to us students about the great need in that country. She said that for every missionary in Belgium, there were 200 in the Belgian Congo. I was really touched by that report and the need in Belgium. That night, the Lord spoke to me in a dream. As He raised a judge's hammer above me, with which I thought He was going to hit me on the head, He said, 'See why I want you to go to Belgium?' This came as a real shock to me, as I had always wanted to go to Africa. However, the Lord had other plans. Interestingly enough, through our work in Belgium, there are now five Belgian couples and a single lady missionary in Africa, accomplishing more than I could have ever done by myself! God's amazing ways!"

And then we had an important visitor.

53. Pastoring Two Churches and God Opening Another Door

Our visitor was the field representative of the Missionary Church denomination. Somehow he had heard about me and now came asking whether I would be willing, for a time, to pastor two of their country churches around Singhampton, Ontario, south of Collingwood. They were waiting for a student to finish seminary in nine months, who would then pastor these churches. We prayed about this and then accepted the offer, as we still had no clear guidance in regards to our future missionary work in Europe. The denomination owned a house in Singhampton, and we moved in there. We were there until June 1969 and had a wonderful time. On Sunday mornings, I'd speak in one church and then drive to the other and preach there. On Sunday evenings, we held a service with the two churches together. Marina taught Sunday school and held Bible clubs.

While in Singhampton, I held evangelistic meetings in several places. I was asked to hold a week of meetings in the Missionary church in Palmerston. Some Dutch people from Drayton attended these meetings and became Christians. One man told me that while milking the cows the next day, he just couldn't stop singing "His Name Is Wonderful." He was truly converted. Another couple told me just recently that they had been at one of those meetings when the lights suddenly went out while I was preaching. Later we heard that a drunk driver had knocked over an electrical pole, cutting the power line. Someone brought me a flashlight, and I kept on preaching. This couple had been so amazed, as they were used to their ministers reading their sermons. While driving home, the husband had said to his wife, "Either we're Christians, or that man is." Later on, they discovered that they were not saved, so they accepted the Lord. It was through these Dutch folks that I held several meetings in Drayton. Some people from Wallenstein Bible Chapel, an Open Brethren Assembly (church), attended. Of course, at that time we didn't know what an important part this church would play in our future. (The words church and assembly will be used alternately. A church is not a building but a group, assembly, of believers).

54. God Leading (Guiding) Us to Our Spiritual Home

When our time in Singhampton was up, we moved with our three lovely daughters, ages 1½, 3½ and five, to a farm house close to Drayton, as we wanted to get to know Wallenstein Bible Chapel (WBC). We had met a number of the people and elders from the church at some of my meetings. One elder had come to me after a meeting, put his finger on my chest, and commented, "You are one of us," meaning that what I believed and taught was what they believed and taught. One of the first meetings we attended at WBC was a Sunday afternoon baptism service. The place was packed, and my wife and I, with our three little girls, sat in the back row. A number of hymns were sung and then two of the elders came to me and said that the speaker had not come, so they asked if I could preach. I told them to sing two more hymns while I went to the back room and asked the Lord for a message. The Lord answered, and I spoke on John 6. I will never forget that day; the Lord gave real liberty.

After that Sunday, everyone knew us. We really felt welcome and believed that this was the church God wanted us to be part of. Shortly after that, we were received into fellowship, which is like membership in other churches. I continued to hold evangelistic meetings and preach at WBC at times. Marina conducted DVBS in the Drayton United Church building. During three weeks of meetings in Clinton, Ontario, some people were saved. One of these was Beryl Gelling, wife of Hank Gelling, who would become a Christian a short while later at some meetings in the USA. After a brief time they were baptized in a river. They would later become our co-workers in Belgium.

At the same time, we were starting to sense God's leading in regards to going to Europe as missionaries. Things were starting to shape up, and Holland and Belgium were coming closer!

In the meantime, we continued our evangelistic and preaching ministry. We also continued to trust the Lord for all our needs and did not make those needs known. We had enough to live on but nothing extra, so when our three little girls asked for tricycles, we prayed. A few days later, we received a phone call.

Our home church in Wallenstein, Ontario.

55. Another Amazing Provision, Showing Our Children that God Is Real

I picked up the phone and heard a woman's voice asking how we were and whether we could use a tricycle. Surprised, I answered, "I think so!" She then asked whether I could come over. When I got there, she took me into the garage. There, amazingly, stood three used tricycles. Unbelievable! I asked how much they would cost, and she said that they were free. I took them home, not showing them to our girls until I had bought some paint and given them a fresh paint job, after which they looked like new. You should have seen our girls—what excitement! We thanked the Lord together and off they went, leaving us with tears in our eyes! Again we had experienced that our God is interested in small things. What a wonderful heavenly Father we have! We continued to minister in the area in different ways, such as holding evangelistic meetings, leading home Bible studies (some with Dutch people), and preaching in assemblies. All this time, the burden on our hearts for Europe continued to grow. At every prayer meeting at WBC, we would ask to pray for Europe.

Finally, we decided to make a trip to Holland to "spy out the land" and see whether and where the Lord would open a door. We left the girls with good friends and then flew to the country I had left more than twelve years before. It was great to see my family and have them meet Marina. My younger brother and his wife had a Volkswagen Beetle, and they drove us all over Holland to visit family, churches, and special meetings. The whole time we were there, we prayed and looked to the Lord to open a door for us. But after four weeks we returned to Canada a bit discouraged, as nothing had opened up. We were starting to wonder whether we were on the right track.

56. Yes to Europe

After returning home and enjoying being with our little girls again, Marina and I began to pray like never before. We were so sure we were to go to Europe, yet nothing had opened up. Had we been wrong? We had worked with the Native people in northern Saskatchewan and wondered if the Lord wanted us there. Several times a day Marina and I would kneel down at our couch and pray, asking the Lord for direction.

One Thursday evening after coming home from a meeting, I said to Marina, "We can't go on like this; we need to know what to do." I took a sheet of paper and drew a line in the middle from top to bottom. On the left side, I listed reasons for staying in Canada, and on the right side, I wrote reasons why we should go to Europe. When I finished, I had three points in the left column and twenty-three in the right. I looked at Marina and said, "What are we praying for? Look at this—it's as clear as can be." The final decision was made; we were now going to start working towards leaving for Europe.

I asked for a meeting with the elders of WBC. Marina and I had decided that if even one of them wasn't in agreement with us going, that we'd not go but would instead wait for further directions. When I met with the elders and told them our desire and decision, some of them smiled. For a moment I thought they were laughing at me. They must have noticed the look on my face, because they explained that they'd smiled because they'd been waiting for us to come to them, as they'd felt for quite some time already that we were to go to Europe. And they were all in agreement! Praise the Lord! The next Sunday we planned to tell the congregation about our plans, but while driving to church that Sunday morning, we had a car accident!

57. God's Protection, So Real!

After a long dry period, it had rained that morning. There must have been some oil or something else that made the road slippery, because as I was passing a car ahead of us, our car swerved around and slid backwards into a shallow ditch, ending up against a farmer's wire fence. It was an absolute miracle that we didn't hit another vehicle ... or horse and buggy, as we were in Mennonite country with lots of buggies on the road. There were cars going both ways, yet we missed them all, and no one was hurt. We got out of the car and saw that a back tire had blown and was flat, which is what had made us swerve. The car wasn't damaged, except for some scratches from the fence. People helped us push the car back on the road; we changed tires and went on to church, where I requested to sing the hymn, "A Thousand, a Thousand Thanksgivings." Strange that this happened on the morning we were going to announce our plans to go as missionaries to Europe. Was it another attempt of the enemy to try to stop us? The Bible teaches that we are in a spiritual battle, even as the Lord Jesus Himself was attacked by Satan before He began His ministry.

I'd been holding evangelistic meetings in different places, including the ... if I may say so ... "well-remembered Moorefield meetings" with lots of people attending. Even now, more than forty years later, I still meet people who talk about these meetings. Children also came along, and Marina would take them aside into a separate room and play her accordion, sing with them, and teach them Bible stories. A number of people and children accepted the Lord, and quite a number received assurance of salvation. It was a great time of blessing and a moving of the Holy Spirit—a foretaste of what later would happen in Belgium. Yet at the same time I wasn't satisfied with what was happening. Something was bothering me ...

58. Called to Plant Churches

Up until now, I had mainly been involved in evangelistic meetings and home Bible studies, at which a number of people had become Christians. When the meetings would finish, I'd move on to another place, leaving the responsibility of teaching these young Christians to others. But Jesus had said that we were to make disciples—not just Christians, but true followers of Him. A verse in the gospel of Matthew burned into my heart. Jesus said, "... I will build My church, and the gates of Hades [hell] shall not prevail against it" (Matthew 16:18b).

When asked why Jesus came to earth, most people answer with, "To show us God's love," or "To reveal God to us," or "To die for our sins." These are all true, but in Matthew, Jesus says that He came to "build his church." What did He mean by that?

In the Old Testament, God used the Jewish people as His instrument. He revealed Himself to them, and they were responsible for passing that revelation on to the world. But they failed, so God set them aside ... at least for the time being. Then Jesus came as God's revelation, and He was the perfect revelation, He could truly say, "He who has seen Me has seen the Father" (John 14:9b). He then went to the cross and paid our debt, so as to be able to forgive us. He rose again to be able to give us new life. All those who receive Him are now children of God, (John 1:12) and together form the (universal) church, which is now God's instrument. This universal church consists of millions of local churches all over the world. We came to realize that God wanted us not just to evangelize, but to build or plant local churches, which would be God's instruments in this sick world. What a challenge! We became aware that God was sending us to Europe to do exactly that. Would that really happen? I wasn't so sure during our first while in Belgium.

59. Preparing to Leave Canada

We now had to decide which mission organization to go with. We'd been praying about this, and still didn't feel the freedom to approach any mission. We discovered that the Open Brethren Assemblies had some 1,500 missionaries all over the world, all without a mission organization. They have Service Committees; for example, there's one in Toronto called Missionary Service Committee (MSC), and another in the US called Christian Missions in Many Lands (CMML). These committees serve the missionaries and the churches. They are recognized by the government and can give tax deductible receipts. They don't have authority over the missionaries, as they believe the missionaries should get their directions from the Lord. We came to believe that the Lord would have us go that way—just with Him, no organization. Later in Belgium, it would become clear why this was so important.

We now knew how we were to go, but we felt we were in need of three things: a strong home church, co-workers, and lots of Christians praying. The Lord had led us to a wonderful church, which had become our spiritual home. We continued to pray that He would provide the right co-workers, and we set out to seek real prayer partners.

Towards the end of October, we packed up and drove out West for the last time before going to Europe. We rented a small house in Herbert, Saskatchewan, and from there I visited assemblies in Saskatchewan and Alberta. I was in Edmonton for a month of evangelistic meetings, while staying with a family that would later move to Belgium and become our first co-workers. We also visited Vancouver, BC and stayed in an apartment that was especially for missionaries. The girls had a great time there, and I visited quite a number of assemblies in and around Vancouver. Everywhere we went, people promised to pray for us and for our future work in Europe. During April 1971, after having said goodbye to Marina's family, we returned to Drayton, Ontario and to WBC to prepare for moving overseas.

60. A Miracle of Healing

As mentioned, in September 1970, Marina and I had been in Holland for four weeks looking for an open door, but nothing had happened. Some time later, we got in contact with my first roommate in Bible college, Henry, and his wife, Lillian, who were ministering with the Bible Christian Union in Holland. They were returning to Canada for a home assignment of six months, and they wrote and asked whether we would be willing to live in their apartment during their absence and help in their church. We felt led off the Lord to accept this, so we started getting ready to move to the Netherlands. About one month before leaving for Europe, Marina became sick with pneumonia, and X-rays revealed a spot on her lungs. I had to go to Peterborough for a week of special meetings. The doctor wanted Marina in the hospital, but she wouldn't leave our girls, so she stayed home. She was very weak, so she just lay on the couch for some of the time. People came to visit, and she told them to help themselves to coffee. Was this another attack of the enemy to keep us from going? I thought so! We had many people all across Canada praying, so when I returned home, I said, "Spot or no spot, we are going."

Four days before we left, X-rays showed the spot was gone. Praise God! ***He is really real.*** Because of her weakness, Marina wasn't able to be at the last Sunday service on June 6, which was also the day we flew to Holland. That morning the Lord gave her Isaiah 45:2–3:

"I will go before you and make the crooked places straight; I will break in pieces the gates of bronze and cut the bars of iron. I will give you the treasures of darkness and hidden riches of secret places."

And the Lord "did go before" us and gave us many, many precious souls in Belgium, "treasures of darkness," who came into the Light.

61. Another Miraculous Provision

On Sunday, June 6, a number of families drove us to the Toronto airport to see us off, which was a great encouragement and blessing. We were stepping out in faith, trusting God to guide us and to meet our every need, and we can testify that He truly was faithful in providing during the thirty-eight years we were in Belgium. It already started before we left. Marina's old accordion was worn out, so there was no use taking it along. About a week before we left, we received a phone call from Toronto. A missionary couple was on their way back to South America, but the dear brother had a stroke, so they had to stay in Canada. They had a beautiful new accordion that he wasn't able to play anymore, so they gave it to us. It was a gift from God. And how it was used in Belgium! There were no other musical instruments at that time, so Marina played it at all meetings.

The God Who is Real

We saw **God being real** when He knew our needs and provided for us at just the right time. Who says believing in God and serving Him is boring? It's the most exciting life to live, even though it's not always easy. We not only saw God provide, but also change the hearts and lives of hundreds and hundreds of people all over Belgium and Europe. I spoke at many conferences in at least twelve different European countries, and I saw God at work again and again!

We were now on our way to Holland, but had Belgium on our hearts; however, we were just letting the Lord lead us step by step. The Lord impressed the words of Hebrews 11:8 on our hearts: "By faith, Abraham obeyed when he was called to go out ... And he went out, not knowing where he was going." He took one step at a time, and so did we. It was exciting, to say the least!

Our family ready to leave for Europe.

62. Experiences in the Netherlands

My family came to get us from the airport close to Amsterdam and took us to the farm of an aunt and uncle in eastern Holland, where we stayed for one week. Amazingly, there were three small bikes there for our girls. Even though I'd been born in Holland, it all felt strange to me, and even more so for Marina and the girls. They started to learn the language, and we had many laughs with that. Praying in Dutch also seemed strange, but the Lord heard us anyway ☺!

We next travelled to our apartment in a town south of Amsterdam, where we lived for about six months. Besides ministering in the small church, we also held a children's Bible club. One morning, Marina woke up with a terribly swollen knee and couldn't walk. I'd lost my voice after entertaining three couples in our home from Friday night until Sunday night, having Bible studies with them and continually talking ... with little sleep. The next day we had Bible club, but Marina couldn't walk and I couldn't talk. With my good legs I carried Marina to the club, and she, with her good voice and in simple Dutch, taught the children, playing her accordion and singing with them. We had a great time!

A niece invited me back to her parents' farm in eastern Holland, where we had stayed before, and held a youth weekend. This time I held three Bible studies a day, which was far too many for the youth, so the next time we did things differently.

In August, Herb and Lillian Schindelka and their four children arrived in Holland on their way to Belgium. I'd stayed with this family while holding special meetings in Edmonton, Alberta. We picked them up at the airport and drove them to Antwerp in

Belgium, where Lillian was from originally. After they settled in, we visited them a number of times, praying and talking together. Slowly we started to sense God's leading.

63. Moving to Belgium

It became clear to the four of us that the Lord was leading us to work together in church planting in Belgium. We now had the three things we had wanted and prayed for: a strong home church, Wallenstein Bible Chapel; many people all over Canada praying for us; and three, gifted co-workers. We were now ready to move to Belgium. Our hearts were thrilled, as this was the place God wanted us to be—Belgium, in Western Europe … in so-called Christian Europe. We knew of people back in Canada who wondered why we'd gone to Europe to be missionaries. Africa needed missionaries, as did Asia and Latin America … but Europe? Had the gospel not come from Europe? Had not many good preachers in North America come from Europe? But someone said once, "No country is as dark as where the light has gone out." Try it out for yourself—a room seems much darker once the light has been on and then turned off. In much of Europe, the light has gone out, especially in the Catholic part.

It didn't take long to find a house to rent in Edegem, a suburb of Antwerp, so on December 23, 1971, we moved from Holland to Belgium. Again it was quite an adjustment. Our co-workers, the Schindelka's, lived about a twenty minute drive from us on the other side of Antwerp. We had gotten in touch with a small assembly in Mechelen, south of Antwerp, and for several months we attended there. At the same time, we started evangelizing in and around Antwerp. Since Lillian Schindelka was born in Belgium, she had contact with her family, and a nephew and his wife became Christians. Herb and I started going from door to door to find out what people in Belgium thought about God and Jesus and so on. Two things really surprised us … or should I say, shocked us.

64. Surprise and Shock

But before I tell you about this, I first want to mention how surprised we were at the Lord's undertaking and provision. We'd left Canada without a salary or a promise of full support. Our home assembly supported us monthly, but that was always less than half of what we needed. Where was the rest going to come from? We had no idea, but we knew we were in the will of God and that He would provide. After having been in Europe for six months, we could truly say that every month enough gifts came in for us, some from people we didn't even know. How wonderful! Praise the Lord! He is faithful and can be counted on.

I feel I need to make something clear. When I speak of the Catholic Church, I'm talking about that church in Belgium or Europe. There are differences between the Catholic Church in Europe, North America, Africa, and other parts of the world. The church in Europe is very liberal, while in Africa it's quite conservative. I think that the North American church is somewhere in between. Also, when I talk about Catholic people, I'm not speaking against them. To the contrary, I love them and I'm very much for them. I've spent much of my life seeking to teach them the Bible and free salvation through the finished work of Christ on the cross. I am, however, upset with the Catholic Church, especially in Belgium and Europe, for having kept people ignorant and in the dark for so long.

So what were the things that shocked us? The first one was the fact that at least 90 to 95 per cent of the people had never seen a Bible. This was unbelievable for a "Christian" country. One of our neighbours told us that her father used to have a Bible, but the local priest had come and taken it. I heard the same story several times. We were told that the Bible was a forbidden book.

There is difference of opinion as to what a number of Church Councils had decreed, but the people understood it to be a Protestant and forbidden book. This has since changed, and now in Catholic schools the children have a Bible, but they are told right from the beginning that the Bible is full of mistakes, so they can't totally trust it. It may surprise or shock you what a seminary professor, who later became a bishop, told me.

65. Unbelievable!

It happened at a home Bible study. About twenty-five Catholic people were present, as was the local priest who had brought this seminary professor along. The priest was upset because some of his people were leaving the Catholic Church. I taught my Bible study, and then after answering some questions, I asked the professor whether he believed the Bible to be the Word of God.

"No," he said, "I believe the Bible contains the Word of God. In other words, there are things in there from God, but there are also many historical mistakes and a lot of scientific nonsense in the Bible, especially in the Old Testament."

I was quiet for a moment, and then explained that Jesus accepted the Bible as the Word of God. Jesus believed in Adam and Eve, in Noah and the flood, and so on. You know what he said? He said, "Oh yes, but Jesus didn't know any better either. He was a child of His times, a first-century man, and in those days they didn't know much about history or science." I can tell you that I became upset and told him that I found it hard to believe that God the Father would allow His perfect Son to teach all kinds of historical mistakes and scientific nonsense. It became very quiet in the room. The Catholic people were shocked at what their professor, who later became a bishop, believed. I realized then what a mission field Belgium was. Much good came out of this meeting, as a number of these folks became true born again Christians.

How different is my faith! I believe the Bible to be the Word of God from cover to cover, and I take it as literally as possible. Notice that I said "as literally as possible." Often it's not possible, such as some of the statements of Jesus: "I am the door" or "I am the true vine." The Bible is living and powerful, able to change lives, and showing that God is real indeed. But there was something else that really shocked us.

66. Spiritual Ignorance

As mentioned before, Herb and I went from door to door to find out what people believed. As we talked to many people, we discovered that people didn't know why Jesus died on the cross. This may seem very strange to you, as Belgium is a Catholic (Christian) country. It may be hard to believe, but it's true. I remember sitting in the living room of an elderly lady who told me she was seventy-five. She also told me that she'd gone to Mass every day of her life, except during the last year, as she wasn't well. Behind her on the wall hung a crucifix, so I asked her whether she believed that Jesus died on the cross.

"Of course," she answered.

I then asked her why Jesus died on the cross. She looked at me and said that she didn't know. I looked at her in utter amazement.

"You've gone to church every day of your life, and you don't know why Jesus died on the cross? Every time you go to Mass you hear the words, 'Behold the Lamb of God, which takes away the sin of the world.'"(John 1:29). She agreed with that, so I asked her what those words meant. She had no idea.

Perturbed, she said, "I haven't studied theology. How should I know?"

I was absolutely dumbfounded and felt like crying. How was this possible? A dear soul having gone to a "Christian" church every day of her life for almost seventy-five years, yet not knowing why Jesus died on the cross ... it was just unbelievable. I met people who told me they believed more in Mary than in Jesus. What a need, and not just in Belgium, but in much of so-called Christian Europe. The light had gone out. I felt once again very confirmed in the fact that God had brought us here. These dear people needed to hear the wonderful gospel of our Lord Jesus Christ. What a mission field!

67. Adjusting

We moved from Holland to Belgium on December 23, 1971. Our two oldest girls, Rosa, age seven, and Lily, age five, seemed to enjoy school in Holland, where they attended for four months. They were quite excited to see Saint Nicholas riding by our house on a horse on December 5, with Black Peter's throwing nuts around. In Canada, Santa Claus comes at Christmas from the North Pole riding a sled pulled by reindeer. In Holland, Saint Nicolas comes on a boat from Spain and then rides around on a horse. Gifts are given on December 5, not on Christmas.

Moving from Canada to Holland was quite an adjustment, but the same was true about moving to Belgium. So many things were different—the mentality, the currency, the stores, the schools, and even the language. Even though approximately six million Belgians speak Dutch, there are French words mixed in, and almost every town or area has a different accent. One can often tell from which part of Belgium a person comes. The two main school systems are the Catholic and the State schools. Our girls went to a State school, as it was so close to where we lived. Even our youngest, Renee, though she was only three, had to go to school, as children in Belgium start at age 2½. Later our girls would be going to a catholic school.

Speaking of children, Antwerp had about a half a million people, and we found out that there was only one Sunday school in the whole city. We went to see one of the teachers, remarking that they must have a lot of children.

"Oh yes," she answered, "we have twenty-six children!"

Marina, with a heart for children, cried, "How is that possible?" Talk about a mission field! And what a challenge! You can well imagine that there would soon be a second Sunday school. And guess where? Our daughters would be getting up early on Sunday mornings to make up their beds and clean their bedrooms so that they could be used as classrooms. What a thrill! And then came April 1, 1972.

68. Joy and Tears

Yes, on Saturday, April 1, we had our first baptism as three people obeyed the Lord. Later, many hundreds would follow. The next day, we started our first little church with sixteen people, children included, in our living room. Fifteen years later, there would be twenty churches all over Flemish-speaking Belgium—some small ones, some large, according to European standards. The Lord blessed in a wonderful way. I was asked to speak at conferences in at least twelve other European countries, as people were so amazed at what was happening in Belgium and they wanted to know what our "secret" was. Of course, we had no secret. It was the work of the Lord. We were there just at the right time. The only tools we had were the Bible, prayer, and, above all, the Holy Spirit, who did the work using weak and frail instruments. Had Jesus not said, "I will build my church?" Psalm 118:23 says, "This was the Lord's doing; it is marvelous in our eyes."

But that didn't mean that it was easy; in fact, I had such a difficult time during the first year that I wondered why the Lord had brought me to Belgium. Thank God that sometime during that year, a friend who had been in Bible college with me was working with a youth movement in Northern Ireland. He asked me to come and speak at a youth weekend with about 300 young people. What a time we had! It was just wonderful to be able to preach in English again to a large group of people. I was overjoyed, and the Lord really worked. Many lives were touched. Even an IRA terrorist was converted, but he had to go into hiding after that.

In spite of all this, I literally wept on the flight home because I was so discouraged. I asked the Lord why in heaven's name He had brought me to Belgium; it was so difficult there. I just wasn't the right person for that kind of country and people. You see, I had three things against me ...

69. God Being Real Doesn't Always Mean No Difficulties

This is actually something personal, but I want to share it with you to give you an idea of why I was feeling so discouraged on the way home from Northern Ireland. You see, I had three things against me. I was a Dutchman, "nen Hollander" as they say in Belgium. The Belgians and Hollanders are not really in love with each other. Most jokes in Holland are about the Belgians, and most in Belgium are about the Dutch. I'm having a hard time withstanding the temptation to tell you some ... ha! I always felt self-conscious about being Dutch. Often, I carried my Canadian passport with me, and when people asked me where I was from, I would tell them that I came from Canada. Their reply was usually, "You speak good Dutch." To this I'd reply, "Well yes, thank you." Eventually they'd ask if I'd ever lived in Holland, and then I had to come out with the truth: "I was born in Holland, but I had nothing to do with that." That would sort of break the ice and they would smile, but I never got over the feeling of being a stranger there, except when people became Christians. Then it changed.

A second obstacle was that I'd never worked with Roman Catholics in Canada, and Belgium was more than 90 per cent Catholic. Why the Lord sent me there, only He knew. I knew very little about the Catholic faith and what they believed, but I learned pretty fast.

Finally, I had never done personal work. I am a preacher—the larger the group, the better it goes. But give me one person and I hardly know what to say. The Bible talks about the gift of evangelism, and both my wife and I have that gift, but while I present the Good News to groups, she does it on a one to one basis. My co-worker, Herb, was also personal, and that's why we teamed up so well. But talk about preaching to large groups in Belgium ...

70. Asking Questions

There were no large groups in Belgium to speak to ... not even with a hundred or ten people. But I'd like to clear something up before I go on. In story #68 I wrote, "I asked the Lord why in heaven's name He had brought me to Belgium; it was so difficult there. I just wasn't the right person for that kind of country and people." In Dutch (Flemish), it was "For that kind of country and 'such' people." As this story has been on Facebook, I received a couple comments asking, "Are we such terrible people?" But that is not what I meant; every nationality has its positive and negative sides. What I meant by "such" people was the fact that they were Catholic, which isn't bad, but I had never worked with these. I hope this will set things straight. We have really come to love these Belgian people, especially all our brothers and sisters in Christ, whom we miss very much!

Because there were no groups to speak to, I had to learn to speak on a one to one basis, which wasn't easy. I eventually learned, even though it never has become easy for me. At the same time, our little church started growing, and our living room started filling up, especially when the children hadn't gone to the bedrooms yet for Sunday school. Operation Mobilization was active in Belgium and held open-air meetings. They gave us the names of people who seemed to show an interest. We would go and visit these folks, but how does one get them interested in a book they've never seen, and of which some were afraid because they'd been told it was a Protestant and dangerous book? But people are curious beings, so we followed Jesus' example and worked on their curiosity. I would ask them if they knew that Jesus had brothers and sisters. Quite shocked, they would ask where that was found in the Bible. I'd show them Mark 6, where it talks about Jesus' four brothers and sisters ... plural. This meant that Mary had at least seven children. It was very interesting to see the expression on their faces. The next question was about ... the Pope!

71. Curious People

I would say the following: "Did you know that Peter, who according to your church was the first Pope, was married?" Again they would ask where that was written, so I'd show them Mark 1:29–31, where Jesus heals Peter's mother-in-law. And when someone has a mother-in-law ...! You should have seen the look on their faces! The Pope married? Some just sat with their mouths open, stunned and not knowing what to say. Don't forget, these people had never heard this before. Very often they would ask, "What else is in the

Bible?" Wow, these are sweet words in the ears of an evangelist and Bible teacher!

I would ask whether it would be alright to come to their house the next week to show them things, and I'd suggest that they invite some relatives and friends who might be interested.

Sometimes when I arrived at their home I'd find eight people present, sometimes twenty-five. I'd give them all a Bible, and we'd start in Mark's gospel. I'd teach for an hour or an hour and a half, have some coffee—of which there was always plenty—and then ask for questions. And there were lots! What does the Bible say about purgatory? Does the Bible really say that Mary had many children? Some found that very difficult. I'd show them Mark 6 again, where it mentions Jesus' brothers and sisters. Some would argue that these were His cousins, so I would show them Matthew 1:25, where it says that Joseph did not know Mary (had no intercourse with her) *until* she had brought forth her firstborn Son. This implies that they did have intercourse afterwards, so brothers and sisters were born. Psalm 69:8 says, "I have become a stranger to my brothers, and an alien to my mother's children." See also Psalm 69:9 and John 2:17. These verses apply to Christ. At times we went until after midnight. Often the question would come: "Who or what are you, anyway?

72. Answering Their Questions

The conversation would go something like this:

"Are you a Roman Catholic?"

"No."

"Are you a Protestant?"

"No, not what you understand as Protestant."

"Are you a Jehovah's Witness?"

"No."

"Well then, what are you?"

"I'm just a Christian. In a sense, I belong to the original catholic (universal) church of Jesus Christ. You know that your church has changed a lot over the last few years. Well, it has changed over the centuries too, and it's hard to know what and who to believe today, as your own priests often disagree with each other. One says there is a purgatory, while another says there isn't. One believes the Pope is infallible, while another says he's just a man like any other. That makes it very difficult to know what to believe. I am someone who says, "Let's go back to the church started by the apostles and described in the Bible."

"Why did you come to Belgium?"

"I came because I believe God sent me here."

"What do you want to do here?"

"My only purpose is to get a Bible to every Flemish person and to get every Flemish person into the Bible. I'd like to study the Bible, God's Word, with you to see what it tells us. I'm not asking you to believe what I say, but what God says in His Word."

"Who is paying you?"

"Since God has brought us here to teach His Word, we believe He'll also provide for us. We have a home church in Canada that looks after about 1/3 of our income; the rest comes from friends and other churches. We never know how much and from whom, yet every month there is enough. It's just wonderful to see how God meets our needs."

My wife and I have lived "out of God's hand" for fifty-six years now, and we've never lacked anything. The Lord has not always given us what we wanted, but He has provided for our needs. It's absolutely amazing! ***How can anyone say that God isn't real?***

73. People Discovering That God Is Real

There was something else that amazed us, even more than God's provision, and that was the change we saw in the people that became Christians. The Bible says that the gospel is "the power of God to salvation" (Romans 1:16). It also says that the Word of God is truth and has power to set free (John 8:31-32). We saw this happening again and again, and it was so wonderful. Often after a Bible study I'd drive home late at night with tears in my eyes, having witnessed again the amazing power of the Word of God. I was so thankful to have been called by God to preach and teach His Word and see what it accomplished! It was beautiful to witness people changing for the good ... people being born again and renewed, and now experiencing the joy of the Lord. They also were discovering that ***God is really real.*** But more of this later.

Let's go back to that first little church, which began on April 2, 1972, in our living room. Even though the first year in Belgium was difficult, people were becoming interested, especially when they saw the changes in the lives of some new converts. The small group began to outgrow our living room, so we started looking for a building to rent. We found one on a street called de Uitbreidingstraat, which means "Expansion Street." Very applicable! We moved into it in 1973.

The year 1972 was very busy. Besides starting a small church in our house, I spoke at several youth weekends in Holland and one in Northern Ireland. We had a group of young people from Holland stay with us for a week of Bible study and training, and we had quite a number of visitors from Canada. During one month, we had more than forty people staying with us for several days and nights. Then Marina had a breakdown.

74. Again, God's Amazing Intervention

With that many visitors and others coming and going, plus Sunday morning and evening services and a weekly Bible study and prayer meeting (all in our house), it was no surprise that Marina went down. The straw that broke the camel's back took place on an evening when I "happened" to be home. Marina was upstairs taking a bath, and I was in the living room reading a book. Marina likes a hot bath, so whenever the water cools down, she drains some and adds fresh hot water. I could hear this from downstairs, but all at once I noticed that the water just kept running. I waited a bit, then went upstairs and knocked on the bathroom door. I got no reply, so I opened the door and found Marina on the floor, unconscious. I picked her up and carried her to the bedroom, finding out how heavy an unconscious person is.

I put her on the bed and called the doctor, who came right away. In Belgium, doctors make house calls. He slapped Marina on the face. I told him not to hit her so hard, but I guess he knew what he was doing. Slowly she came to; was I ever relieved! After checking the bathroom and talking together, we discovered what had happened. We had the kind of hot water heater that heats the water with a gas flame. The burned gas goes outside through an exhaust pipe. That night there was a storm, and the wind was right on our house, blowing the burned gas back into the bathroom. Marina, not feeling well, got up to get out of the bath. She fainted and fell on the floor. The doctor, who knew us quite well, told Marina not to entertain any more visitors. He prescribed her some medication and told me to take her to the park every day and walk with her to regain her strength. And so we did. It was a new experience for us, as on the prairies in Saskatchewan people don't go walking ☺. Just think what could have happened had I not been home that evening! Someone had kept me at home. **Is God real or not?**

75. Another Amazing Provision

Marina slowly regained strength, and the small assembly grew. However, there was a problem. Many people in those days didn't have a car. Quite a few lived some distance from our meeting place and had to be picked up. Our car, like most others, was quite small and couldn't hold very many people. Several families had quite a number of children, so we had to drive twice or have two cars go to pick them up. Marina and I started asking the Lord to provide a Volkswagen bus so that we could transport more people at one time. Of course, we didn't have the money for this. We had our car as a trade-in, and we had some money saved, but we were $1,000 short, which was a lot of money in 1972.

We continued to pray and received the assurance that the Lord would provide in some way. I went to the dealership and, by faith, ordered the bus. It would be about two weeks before we could get it. A whole week went by, but nothing happened. One week before picking up the bus, we received a letter from good friends in Canada. They'd been in a bad car accident, and the insurance covered all their expenses with a little left over. They didn't need all the money, so when the husband came home from work that day, he'd told his wife that God had led him to send the money to us. His wife replied that she had felt the same way. *They knew nothing about our need* or our prayers to God for help. Enclosed with the letter was a cheque for $1,000. Amazing! We praised the Lord and thanked Him for His undertaking, and that He'd put it on the hearts of our friends to send us this money *just at the right moment!* Time and again the Lord provided, sometimes in little ways, and at other times in big ways. Absolutely amazing! Do you think there is a God? **Do you think He is real?**

76. God Changing Lives

In story #73, I wrote this: "But there was something else that amazed us, even more than God's provisions, and that was the change we saw in the people that became Christians." I would just love to give you example after example of dear people who accepted the Lord and were born again and the change we saw in their lives, but space does not permit. Besides, I might miss some folks, and they may wonder why I left them out. So without using names, I will just mention a few.

We came in contact with a family with four children. The mother was very interested and had been listening to the evangelical TV broadcast from Holland. I believe that through it she had accepted the Lord. We were invited to her home, and a little later a Bible study was started there with seven or eight people, of which two couples were neighbours. The lady of the house who had accepted the Lord also started coming to our Sunday meetings, bringing her children along. Her husband had no real interest and was taken up with sports on Sunday mornings, but he did attend the home Bible study.

One night I was teaching about the need to be born again. He laughed and said, "If I ever get born again, it will have to be caesarean," which made all of us laugh. After quite some time, he did accept the Lord and even started coming on Sunday morning. Much later he became an elder in the Antwerp church and was a godly leader. He and his wife were also very involved in our camp work. It was wonderful to see how ***real God's work was*** in their lives. Not only did they become true Christians, but they grew in the Lord and became effective instruments in His hands.

A couple of the neighbours also became Christians, but one man kept resisting. We continued to pray for him and asked the Lord to deal with him. One Saturday evening he phoned, and with a trembling voice asked me to come over right away, which I did.

77. New Christians Obeying the Lord

When he let me in, I noticed that his face was very white. He told me right away that he'd been in two car accidents that day. In the morning, he had rolled his car, which was a total wreck, and in the late afternoon he'd crashed another car. Amazingly he wasn't hurt … unbelievable! But it had scared him to death, as it could have been deadly. He was now ready to give his life to God and accept the Lord Jesus. Wonderful! Sometimes God uses drastic measures to bring people to their knees and draw them to Himself.

What happened after people became Christians? It was wonderful to work with young converts who knew nothing about the Bible. After they accepted the Lord they would often ask, "What do we do now?" I would tell them to read the book of Acts and see what the new Christians did in the days of the apostles. The next time we met, I'd ask them what they had learned. Often with a sort of sheepish look on their face they'd answer, "They got baptized."

"Well, what are you waiting for?" I'd ask, smiling.

In time, a baptism service would be planned. Their willingness to obey the Lord showed that they were truly converted. Since we believed that the Bible teaches baptism by immersion, and we didn't have a tank in our building, we went to other churches, and even a private swimming pool. One time we went with a large group to Brussels to have a baptism in a French speaking assembly. Whereas here in North America people often hug family and friends when they meet, in some European countries they kiss each other. In Belgium, people kiss three times: first on one cheek, then on the other, and then again on the first. At the entrance of this assembly stood a nice looking young lady who greeted everyone who came in!

78. Meeting and Experiencing God Together

We had friends visiting us who came along to the baptism. As the man entered the building, the young woman greeted him the Belgian way, with three kisses. We had a good laugh and a wonderful baptism service, with much joy and praise to God for what He had done in the lives of these new believers.

After people were baptized, we again directed them to the book of Acts and together discovered that the new Christians in those days met together on the first day of the week for the "breaking of bread" (Acts 20:7). So we also started meeting on Sunday mornings with a small group around our table with a loaf of bread and a cup of wine on it. We would sing some songs as Marina played her accordion. After some singing, the children would go to our bedrooms for Sunday school. In the beginning, we only had two classes, which were taught by Marina and our co-worker's wife. One Sunday, Marina had twelve little ones in a small bedroom ... quite crowded!

We would continue the meeting with prayer, a scripture reading, another prayer, a song, another scripture, and so on as people felt led to participate. Then someone would give thanks for the bread and pass it around; someone would give thanks for the cup and it was passed. After that, a message from the Bible was given. It was all so simple and yet so beautiful. The Lord blessed, and more came to Him as the Spirit was free to move.

In our home Bible studies, I started teaching some things that really shocked some of the Catholic people!

79. You're Sure You're Going to Heaven?

In the first year or two, I used the gospel of Mark in home Bible studies. After a while, I felt I needed something else, so I made up ten topical Bible studies from the first three chapters of the Gospel of John. Some of the topics were: How Do We Know

There Is a God? What About the Bible? What About Sin? The Lamb of God. After the study on sin, people usually felt pretty guilty, which was good, because now they wanted to know about the solution. I used John 1:29 to explain the gospel: "Behold! The Lamb of God who takes away the sin of the world!"

The first surprise they got was the fact that we are not saved by doing good works, something all religions except true Christianity teach, even though they differ on what comprises "good works." They all say, "Do something," while the gospel says, "It is done." Forgiveness is a gift of God. Eternal life is a gift, paid for by Jesus on the cross, where He cried out, "It is finished," (John 19:30) or "It is done." Often I would get this reaction: "You mean to say that we don't need to do anything?"

"Correct, except to acknowledge your sin and accept Jesus, God's gift."

The second surprise was the fact that we can be sure of going to heaven. When I'd ask people if they believed they would go to heaven when they died, the answer was usually, "I hope so." To this I'd respond, "Well, I know so. I am 100 per cent sure that I'm going to heaven when I die." They'd look at me in amazement and often say, "You think you're better than us?" I would answer, "No, it has nothing to do with being better; I know that I'm just as sinful as anyone else, but I also know that Jesus died for my sin. I have accepted Him, and God has accepted me."

The third surprise or shock came when I showed them some passages in the letter to the Hebrews!

80. The Beauty of God's Salvation

It was just wonderful to have a room full of people, sometimes fifteen, twenty-five, forty, and even seventy ready to listen to God's Word, which was totally new to them. It was quite a revelation for them to hear that forgiveness and eternal life are a gift from God, received by faith without any works. On top of that, they discovered that we can be sure of this. They were so surprised to hear me say that I was sure I would go to heaven when I died. As I explained the gospel to them, I took them to Hebrews 10:5: "Therefore, when He [Jesus] came into the world, He said: 'Sacrifice and offering You [God] did not desire, but a body You have prepared for Me.'" The writer goes on to say, "Then He said, 'Behold, I have come to do Your will, O God.' He takes away the first that He may establish the second" (Hebrews 10:9). This is one of the most important verses in the New Testament.

What is meant by *the first*? It's referring to the Old Testament temple, with its altar, its sacrifices, its priests, and its ceremonies. When Jesus died on the cross, the veil of the temple was torn from top to bottom, an indication from God that He was finished with all of that. And why? *"He takes away the first that He may establish the second."* And what is *the second*? It is Jesus' own sacrifice on the cross, which was so perfect and so complete, no other sacrifice ever has to be brought again. He died **once for all**. The Catholic Church is still very much in the Old Testament. It has a temple (the church building), and an altar and daily sacrifices (the Mass, priests, and ceremonies). Although God was finished with "the first," the Jews didn't accept it, so they restored the veil and went right on. But then come those shocking words in verse 11: "And every priest stands ministering daily and offering repeatedly the same sacrifices, which can never take away sins." This is speaking of the Jewish priests, but my Catholic listeners took it to mean their priests. So what now?

81. My Stay in the Maternity Ward

I explained to them that God no longer dwells in church buildings made by hands (Acts 17:24), but that He now lives in every individual believer (1 Corinthians 6:19) and in all believers together, called "the church" (1 Corinthians 3:16). Peter says that we, if we are true believers, are being built up as a spiritual house (temple) and a holy (royal) priesthood (1 Peter 2:5, 9). In Revelation 1:6 and 5:10, John says that Jesus has made us priests. This, of course, was a tremendous surprise for these dear people—to hear that if they truly accepted the Lord Jesus, they would be priests. Unbelievable! I told them not to tell their family or friends, because they might think that something had gone wrong with them ☺. Imagine, for a Catholic person to say "I am a priest!" Yet that is true and it's what the Bible teaches.

While still living in Antwerp, something happened on a Saturday afternoon. You may remember that I'd dislocated my right shoulder several times, twice in Bible college and once in California. Well, on this Saturday afternoon in Antwerp, I dislocated my shoulder again. This time, I couldn't get it back in myself, so Marina phoned my co-worker, who took me to a Catholic hospital close by, which was run by nuns. They put me out, put the shoulder back in place, and told me to stay overnight. But the only free bed was in the maternity ward!

82. Humour

So there I lay, in the only free bed in the whole hospital ... in the maternity ward. Now many of you have been there, as you were born there, but I wasn't. My birth took place in my grandparents' house, so it was quite an experience for me and for the nuns, who thought it was hilarious! I had a fairly good sleep. After breakfast the next morning I cleaned up and the nuns got me to sit up. Then two of them came in, one holding a baby from a mother in the next room, who gladly "loaned" her baby to me. The nun put the baby in my arms, and there I sat with a grin on my face while the other nun took a picture. They laughed and laughed; in fact, after they went out I heard the whole ward laughing. A little later I was allowed to go home with my arm in a sling, and a box full of things for mothers who had just given birth ☺.

It was good to be home again. I couldn't drive a car, but I was able to continue leading Bible studies and preaching. My dear wife, after having recovered quite a bit from her breakdown, was not only busy with household duties and helping our children with their school work, but also spent a lot of time preparing Sunday school materials, as there was little of that in Belgium. She also helped some of the young converts, training them to teach our growing Sunday school. Marina is not an artist, but she drew interesting pictures for her preschool class, like Zacchaeus climbing into a tree, and Jesus coming and saying, "Come down, I'm going to your house." She did have problems with the language at times and would use a wrong word. One day she told a neighbour lady that she was having a baby, which was coming out of her nose! ☺.

83. Language Laughter

Marina had some interesting experiences, especially with learning the language. She did really well learning Dutch during the six months we were in Holland, but when we moved to Belgium, she had to start learning again. They speak many dialects there, and even though the Flemish is Dutch, quite a few French words and phrases are mixed in, as part of Belgium is French speaking. She had difficulties with some of the Dutch words that were similar yet meant something different. There were, for example, words such as *vallen* = falling, but *valling* = having a cold. This word is only used in Belgium and southern Holland. Another such word was gevallen = fallen, *te vallen* = to fall, and *bevalling* = having a baby.

One day I was in the kitchen when the doorbell rang. Marina was in the living room and went to the door. She had a terrible cold at the time, with red, teary eyes and a running nose. She opened the door and saw our neighbour lady standing there. Looking at Marina, she said, "What's the matter with you?" Marina answered, "I have a *bevalling* (I'm having a baby), and it's coming out of my nose." I heard this and thought I was going to die laughing ☺! There have been similar incidents, which make life interesting and sometimes a bit embarrassing.

We continued with evangelism and home Bible studies, and more and more people became true born again Christians. Lives were being changed, which was so good to see. The little church kept growing; it was really amazing and exciting to see God working in the hearts and lives of people. Of course, there were problems too—broken marriages and broken homes, ruined lives, and other issues. In some cases, we saw miracles happen, lives changed, and marriages restored, all due to the fact that people surrendered to the Lord and became obedient to Him. But we were not able to help everyone, and this was at times heartbreaking and caused sleepless nights. Eventually, a door opened to start a second work in a town east of Antwerp called Beerse. How exciting!

84. Growth of God's Work

A group of young people from Holland stayed with us for a week of Bible study, prayer, and evangelism. The girls used two bedrooms on the third floor of our house, while the fellows slept in our church building. After Marina had a breakdown, her younger sister, Carol, came from Canada and stayed with us for about six months. She was a tremendous help. Several times we went to Beerse with the team to go from door to door. It resulted in a few contacts, with whom we followed-up. Christians in Antwerp also had some connections in Beerse, and Operation Mobilization had done some evangelism there and gave us the name of a couple willing to open their home for a weekly Bible study. Thus, the first step was taken. I started driving to Beerse every week for this study and some visitation.

In the meantime, the work in Antwerp continued to grow. We had quite a large Sunday school. Even Carol, who didn't speak Dutch, helped out, as did our oldest daughter, Rosa, who was nine years old. In the old building, which with a lot of work we had fixed up to use as a church, the preschool children met in a small kitchen. There must have been about twenty-four of them—a crowded place indeed! A little boy approximately three years old was very proud of his father's big Bible and took it into the dry-cleaning store where his mother worked, showing it to people and saying, "Daddy's Bible says that God cares for you." He had learned this in Sunday school. We also had the joy of seeing a prostitute come to know the Lord and stop her activities. People who have never been involved in starting a new church, especially with all young converts, have no idea of the joy and excitement experienced! *And ... the presence of God being so real.*

85. Activity and God's Faithful Provision

We're now into 1974. I trust you understand that it's not easy to remember everything of these last forty years, considering all that went on: we planted about twenty-four churches; we started a summer camp ministry for children and youth; I spoke in at least forty conferences in more than twelve European countries; we went on furlough to Canada at least ten times for periods of two to eight months, one time staying 2½ years and helping to start a new church there; I spoke in churches and conferences in Canada and the US; I recovered from two heart attacks, a back operation, and burn out; and Marina almost died but received a pacemaker just in time. Not to mention the five times we moved in Belgium, where every house, except the last one, had to be fixed up, taking from one to four months of work. Plus all the buildings we worked on to become usable as churches ...

One thing I want to mention here is God's loving care for us all those years. For example, it was really amazing to see that when the value of the dollar went down, our support went up, and vice versa ... all without our supporters in Canada realizing what was going on. When we arrived in Belgium, we didn't have that much support, but because the value of the dollar was so high, we had enough. Before we left Belgium, we had much more support, but because the dollar had really gone down (from seventy Francs to twenty-four), we had about the same as in the beginning. AMAZING! These were all wonderful, and at times miraculous, provisions from the Lord. ***Yes, God is real!*** Hallelujah!

86. An Interesting Visit

Now, for a moment, we need to back up a little to the fall of 1973. It had been a year and a half since the Antwerp church was started, and it was doing really well and growing. Both my co-worker and I held home Bible studies, and people were being saved, baptized, and welcomed into the church. It was wonderful to see. I had also started a Bible study in Beerse, a town about thirty-five kilometres east of Antwerp. A couple had agreed to open their home for a study. The man, André (not real name), witnessed to his employer, who, together with his wife, started attending. André and his wife talked to a young woman on the train, and she started attending. This lady in turn talked to some friends, a young couple, about this "new faith," as some called it.

I visited this couple in their home on a Monday evening when the Jehovah's Witnesses were there. I have met with J.W.'s many a time, and always told them that we would only discuss two things: Was and is Jesus really God? And, What must we do to receive eternal life? That evening, they showed a number of Bible texts that talk about Jesus' humanity. I then showed a whole lot more about His deity. The first verse I focused on was Isaiah 44:6, where God says that He is the First and the Last. In the book of Revelation, John says that Jesus is the First and the Last. They had no idea what to do with that. Then I shared Isaiah 44:8, where God says that He is the Rock and there is no other. In the New Testament, Jesus is called the Rock. Since there is only one Rock ... After some discussion, they became very upset and left. I stayed and explained the gospel to the couple and then drove home. The next evening, I went back to bring them a Bible, as they didn't have one. I rang the doorbell, and the woman appeared at the door with a big smile on her face.

87. New Christians

I looked at Mieke (not real name) and asked, "How are you?"

"Really good," she answered. "Last night after you left, my husband and I talked until 2:00 a.m., and then we prayed and accepted Jesus."

"Well, that's wonderful," I replied. "And how did things go today?"

"Oh, very good," she answered. "But you know, Richard, at my work do people ever swear."

Then I was the one to smile. "Well, isn't that something ... that they just started doing that today?"

She looked at me with wide-open eyes and began to laugh. I explained to her that they had been doing this all the time, but she'd never heard it. Now that the Holy Spirit had come to live within her, her ears had been opened. I told her also that there would be more surprises yet. Some time later I started a Bible study in their home, as they were living in another town. Her sister and husband became interested and attended; they, in turn, talked to friends, who also started coming.

I had rented a hall in Beerse and held two evangelistic meetings there, each time showing a Moody science film followed by me preaching. A young man, Jeff (not real name), was there and started coming to the Bible studies at André's; he brought his girlfriend along, and a little later another friend. In the meantime, Mieke's husband had talked to his brother in Eastern Belgium, in the province called Limburg, and I was invited to their home. I will come back to this shortly, but as you can see, "the ball really started rolling." It was so exciting to meet these interested and curious people. God was at work! Then a colleague of Mieke talked to her about his wife, who was having a hard time and had come to the point of wanting to commit suicide. In fact, one day while he was at work, she left a note for her husband and walked to the canal.

88. Suicide Intentions and God's Miraculous Intervention

Marianne (not her real name) walked slowly while all kinds of thoughts and memories raced through her head: her father's death when she was nine, her mother trying to raise five children by herself and then re-marrying, the painful relationship with her stepfather, the terrible times of depression, getting a job as a teacher but not able to handle a class of thirty mentally challenged children from ages six to twelve, getting married, having many things go wrong, having a serious nervous breakdown ... it was all too much. Why continue? Life wasn't worth living. She had no energy left, her life was in ruins, and there was only despair. Her only thought now was how to end it.

As she drew close to the canal, a small piece of newspaper blew over the ground. She picked it up. The first words (by accident?) were, "Is there life after death?" All at once fear set in—the fear of dying. Was it because of her Catholic upbringing, or the lessons in religion she herself had given to her students about God's existence? Whatever it was, it kept her from jumping into the canal. How long she sat there thinking she can't remember, but she got up and started walking. Halfway home she met her husband, who for the first time ever had left work early, and had found her suicide note and came looking for her. That night in bed fear overwhelmed her and she cried out to God. The next morning, two Jehovah's Witnesses came to her door, causing even more confusion. She decided to go along with her husband to a meeting in a hall in town where a film was going to be shown and someone would be talking about the Bible. The film was about a pilot who crashed his plane because instead of following his instruments, he followed his own feelings. What a lesson! Then a man got up and began to speak about revolution. Her husband whispered, "We're in the wrong place here; this guy is a communist!"

89. Revolution in Our Hearts Makes God Real

Marianne looked at her husband, who through all the difficulties had stayed true to her, and said, "I'd really like to hear what he has to say." He agreed and they stayed. The speaker said that before continuing, he wanted to go back to the film for just a few comments. He explained that one of the most important things

The God Who is Real

a pilot has to learn is "flying blind," which means that he's not to go by his feelings, but by the instruments on the panel in front of him. When pilots are flying through thick mist or clouds, they lose their feeling, or sense, of direction. One of them may say that they are climbing, while the other will disagree and argue that they are descending. The speaker applied this to people who seem to be flying through a mist and have lost their sense of direction. One will say that there is a God, while another will disagree. One will believe that there is life after death, while another argues that death is the end. Who do we listen to when there are so many opinions? But God has given us a dashboard with instruments—the Bible—and we need to heed that.

Then the speaker, who was actually me, changed the subject. I knew that there were a number of younger people present who had communistic ideas. I told them that I wanted to speak about a word that could very well be the most important one in their dictionary: "Revolution." Many nodded approvingly! I said that I had looked up the word and found two very good definitions. The first was, "Revolution, a total rotation or turn around." Again nods of approval. The second was, "Revolution is the overthrow of the present government and the establishing of a new one." Many cheered!

"I agree wholeheartedly with you," I said. "What we need is a total turn around, the overthrow of the present government, and the setting up of a new one. There's only one point on which we differ …!"

90. Why and What Revolution?

I saw many curious looks as they wondered what was coming. "I agree with you," I repeated, "we need a total turn around, the overthrow of the present government, and the setting up of a new one. The only thing we differ on is where this should take place. You say it should take place in the capital, Brussels, while I say right here (pointing at my chest), in our hearts. We need a total turn around here, the overthrow of the present 'I' government, and the setting up of the government of Jesus Christ. This is what will change us and the world. When man was originally created under God's government, he rebelled and resisted God's government, setting up his own. 'Self' became and still is the ruler. And there are so many 'self's' or 'I's' in the world, all wanting to be number one. That's what's wrong with this world, and the only way to really change it is to turn back to God and allow Him to be King. Man's rebellion has separated him from God, from the source of all good.

Thank God, He didn't give up on us, but continued to love us and sent His Son to pay for our sins and remove the wall of separation." As I was speaking, I quoted John 3:16, which none of them had ever heard. "The Bible says that God so loved the world that He gave His only begotten Son, that whoever believes in Him should not perish, but have everlasting life."

I explained a little more, not knowing that Marianne, hearing these words, accepted Jesus right there and then, and a miracle happened in her heart and life. "He gave me a new heart and a new mind," she later told me. I thought of what had happened in Cornelius' house in Acts 10 when Peter preached and the ones who were listening received Jesus. How wonderful to see this repeated! How is it with you, dear reader? Has there been a revolution in your heart?

91. The Power of Changed Lives

Besides the church in Antwerp, there were now also two weekly Bible studies, one in Beerse and one in a town about eight kilometres east. It was amazing how more and more people came to know the Lord, especially family members and friends of the people in the second study. Yet we didn't do any "evangelism" as it's usually done. We no longer went from door to door, and we didn't have tent meetings or campaigns, except for a couple of film evenings. How then did people come? They came because of the ones who had come to know the Lord. Let me put it this way: the changed lives of the truly converted people drew the attention of others, who then became interested. The most powerful testimony on earth and the most powerful witness is the changed life of a truly converted person, someone who has surrendered to the Lord Jesus and is filled with His Spirit and joy. ***His or her life shows that God is real indeed!***

How does this come to pass? It happens through the power of the Word of God, and the Spirit of God Who works in answer to prayer. My wife and I had been praying for years, and I had also spent many, many hours praying with a friend. Besides that, we had a wonderful home church in Canada with many praying people. We also travelled through a large part of Canada, everywhere visiting churches and encouraging people to pray for our upcoming ministry in Europe. Once in Belgium, we started preaching the Word of God, and I discovered again the power of

God's Word—not only in meetings, but also when speaking personally to people. I remember visiting a Catholic lady and asking her whether she read the Bible. She said she didn't, but she prayed a lot all day. I showed her Proverbs 28:9: "One who turns away his ear from hearing [reading] the law [God's Word], even his prayer is an abomination." I said to her very quietly, "When you don't read God's Word to listen to Him, He will not listen to you; in fact, your prayers offend Him." I saw her face turn white as the Holy Spirit pricked her heart.

92. The Amazing Power of God's Word

Two weeks later after some Bible studies and serious talks, she accepted the Lord Jesus into her heart and became a true born again Christian! Yes, the Word of God is powerful! Jeremiah 23:29 says, "'Is not My word like a fire?' says the Lord, 'And like a hammer that breaks the rock in pieces?'" I have seen hardened hearts broken before the Lord and come to Jesus. I have seen God's Word burning up arguments, and hearts humbled and bowed before Him. In Ephesians 6:17, Paul says that the Word of God is like a sword that cuts into hearts, as it did on the day of Pentecost when Peter preached in the power of the Holy Spirit that God had raised up the Jesus whom they had crucified. People were "cut to the heart" and came to repentance and faith. I saw this happen with this woman. How wonderful to experience the power of God's Word. And I have witnessed this happen time and again.

Many a time when talking to people, I've asked them if they were Christians. When they answered "yes," I then asked them if they read the Bible. Almost always the answer would be "no." I would then show them John 8:47, where Jesus says, "He who is of God hears [reads] God's words; therefore you do not hear [read], because you are not of God." Many a time I have seen the Holy Spirit cutting these folks to the heart (Acts 2:37).

But now back to Beerse. As a number of people became Christians, it became evident that a church should be started here. One evening when we were together with a good group of young believers, we talked about this and the need for a building in which to meet. We had a time of prayer, and then someone mentioned that the old windmill close to the centre of the town was up for rent. An old dilapidated windmill as a church building?

93. A Church in an Old Windmill?

A new church in Beerse? It had been on my heart for some time. Don't forget, we believed that the Lord had led us to Belgium to build churches, not buildings. Even though buildings became necessary too, our focus was on building gatherings or assemblies of true born again believers. The words of Jesus in Matthew 16:18b were always on my mind: "… I will build my church and the gates of Hades shall not prevail against it." My constant prayer was, "Lord, build your church." I firmly believed that this was the purpose for our being in this country. I was also convinced that planting churches was the best and fastest way of evangelizing the world. Notice the apostle Paul's ministry, and also Christ's description of Christians as the salt of the earth and the light of the world (Matthew 5:13–14). My heart was thrilled when people in and around Beerse became Christians. Through these

Christians, I came in contact with people further east in the province of Limburg, but that is for later.

We went to talk to the owner of the mill, who gave us the key to go and look at it. The sails/blades had been taken off, but the large round tower was still there. The mill was several storeys high and included a good sized round room on the main floor, as well as a large hall that could seat close to 200 people. There were also living quarters—a house with two bedrooms. But the whole place was in bad shape, and a lot of fixing-up would have to be done, yet we saw that it had tremendous potential. We looked at the place a couple of times, and after much prayer, we agreed to rent it. The next Monday morning I drove from Antwerp to sign the contract and get the key from the owner. I went to the mill feeling excited that this was now ours. With a happy heart, I walked into the building, but became suddenly and utterly shocked.

The famous old windmill where so much happened.

94. God's Speaking, So Real!

The times we'd looked at the mill before renting it had been nice days, or at least dry days, but that day it was pouring rain. It seemed to come down in buckets. I parked the car and ran in to avoid getting too wet. Once inside, I looked around and could hardly believe what I saw. There was water almost everywhere. Small puddles dotted the large hall, while water dripped from the ceiling. In the round room, the water ran down the walls. I went into the house, where the water wasn't coming from above, but from below. Groundwater was slowly creeping up the walls. It all looked sickening! I walked around and took another look. My happiness was gone in no time, and a terrible sadness and discouragement settled in. I had no desire to see any more, so I left the building and drove home very depressed, wondering whether we had made a mistake in renting this place.

Once home, I told my wife about it, and she was shocked too. I went upstairs to my study and sat down in a daze. But then the thought came to take God's Word. I was reading in the Dutch Bible in Micah and came to chapter 2, where the last sentence of verse 12 hit me right on. It looked like it was written in bold: "Het zal er gonzen van mensen" (NBG). The English Bible says, "The place will throng with people" (NIV). The Dutch word *gonzen* means "buzz" or "hum," much like the sound one hears standing close to a beehive. I instinctively knew this was for me; this was God's word for me at this time. You may wonder how I knew that. Well, I just knew. There was that inner witness of the Spirit. Sure enough, in the years to come, this word would be fulfilled as hundreds of people again and again were present to see many, many new Christians baptized in that mill. But some strange things also happened at times at those baptisms!

95. The Place was "Buzzing" as Promised

I'm fast forwarding for a moment. When these baptisms took place, the strangest stories were told by some of the townspeople. I heard that a rumour was going around that we were baptizing people naked behind a sheet that was being held up. Imagine! Well, I can assure you that never happened. The closest we ever came to that occurred when someone forgot to tell a young man who'd recently become a Christian what to wear when baptized. We didn't use special gowns, but told folks that they were saved in plain clothes, so we would baptize them in plain clothes. But someone had slipped up, so imagine my surprise when this young man came out of the dressing room in his swimming trunks. I looked at my co-worker with a question mark all over my face, but the man was in the water already being baptized. I'm quite sure the angels in heaven smiled.

Another time, an elderly man who had been gloriously saved after leaving the Catholic Church feeling totally disillusioned, came to be baptized. Once again, nobody had instructed him, and he came out of the dressing room in beautiful striped pyjamas! No problem. I believe the angels smiled again, rejoicing in the fact that an old sinner had been saved and was being obedient to the Lord. But when he started coming up out of the water, I noticed that the elastic in his pyjama pants wasn't tight enough, and I saw his wet pants slowly going down. I jumped over and grabbed him with one hand, and his pants with my other, and everything was fine. We all rejoiced. Oh, those baptisms were wonderful times! The most we ever baptized in one afternoon was thirty-four, praise the Lord. They were feasts, with buns and coffee afterwards, and what a "buzzing," just as I'd been told. We believe that the Bible teaches that baptism is a picture of us being buried with Christ and resurrected to new life, and that immersion is the best picture of this. You may not see it that way, and that's okay. We have our convictions and respect others who hold to different views.

96. God Taking Us Further East

We must now go back a bit to the winter of 1973/74. We were still living in Edegem, a suburb of Antwerp. The church in Antwerp was growing and doing well. My co-worker was doing a great job, while I was still active in that assembly too, but at the same time turning my attention eastwards towards Beerse and even further. I now had two Bible studies in the Beerse area, and I'd also started two studies in the eastern province of Limburg. These had come about through contacts of a young couple close to Beerse. The man had a friend in a town called Peer, to whom he introduced me, and he also had an older brother a bit further south. The brother and his wife invited me to their home. When I arrived, I met another couple, friends whom they had invited to be present.

It turned out to be a very interesting evening as I explained the Bible to them. We actually had a Bible study, which was totally new to them. It must have lasted around three hours. Eventually I mentioned that I needed to go home, as I had at least an hour and a half drive ahead of me. I asked permission to close the evening with prayer, as I did in every home I was invited to. Never has that been refused! I prayed, and when I was finished it was very quiet. They looked at me, not knowing what to say. I believe the Holy Spirit had touched their hearts; in fact, I know He had, because the lady friend told me later that as I was praying, she knew this was it—this was what she needed. That same evening, she accepted the Lord. I wanted to get up, but all at once the questions came. Why did you not make the sign of the cross? Why did you not pray the Lord's Prayer and Hail Mary? It took another hour to explain all that. Some time later I visited the couple in Peer, and that visit was just as interesting … maybe even more so.

97. Night Shift

When I left the home where I had met the two couples, the lady, let's call her Leen, who later told me she had accepted the Lord that night, asked me to come to their home. She offered to invite relatives and friends. I'll come back to this later. That night I drove home almost all the way with tears in my eyes, just praising and thanking the Lord for calling me into this ministry. What a joy to teach and preach His Word to people who had never seen a Bible and had never heard the true gospel, and to be able to present such a wonderful message. I felt so privileged! **God was so real!** I got home well after midnight, which wasn't unusual. Most of the time I got in at 1:00, 2:00, or 3:00. A few times it was even 4:00 and 5:00 in the morning. But it was worth it! In the years to come, I would see so many come to know Him, so many transformations, so many happy faces. What a joy, not only for me, but also in heaven (Luke 15).

Some time later, I went with the young couple from close to Beerse to visit their friends in Peer. The names of these friends are Martin and Lydia Symons. I have permission to use their names, and I'll tell you in a moment why. What an evening it was! They were good Catholic people, but like so many others, a bit confused over the many changes taking place in the Catholic Church, even though this church had always claimed to be the one and only true, unchanging church. The questions kept coming, and I showed them the answers in the Bible. I had no idea at that time that I was in the home of two wonderful people who, in time, would become our first Flemish full-time workers. That's why I'm allowed to use their names. It was late when we left their apartment and drove to Beerse and then on to Antwerp, where a very important decision was going to be made.

98. An Interesting Conversation

Before I say anything more about this important decision, let me tell you about the next visit with Martin and Lydia in Peer. This time there was a Catholic priest present. I liked the man and found him very sympathetic and honest, but we discovered that he knew very little about the Bible. I asked him if he knew that Jesus had brothers and sisters. He didn't, so I showed him several scriptures that he'd never seen before. I also asked him if he knew that Peter, who was the first Pope according to his belief, was married. He was very surprised, and I showed him Mark 1, where Jesus healed Peter's mother-in-law, which of course meant that he was married. We went on like that for a while, and then he admitted that in seminary they had never really studied the Bible that much, but rather books about the Bible. I really appreciated his honesty. It was late again when I left the house. Some time later, a Bible study was started in the Peer area, and also one a bit further south in Zolder.

Because of these studies in Limburg and in the Beerse area, I had to do a lot of driving. This, plus the fact that the work in Antwerp was doing great, begged the question of whether or not we should move. We believed the Lord had brought us to Belgium to start churches. In fact, when my future co-worker from Canada, Hank Gelling, was visiting us, he came along to a prayer meeting where we prayed and asked the Lord to start ten churches in ten years. Hank couldn't believe what he heard, but the reality is that not ten churches were started in ten years, but twenty in fifteen years! God was at work, and we were privileged to be part of that. We sought the Lord as to a possible move and the starting of a new church in Beerse. How would He lead? Excitement was growing!

99. Move?

We prayed, but at the same time we worked hard, not only holding Bible studies and visiting people, but also fixing up the mill in Beerse to get it ready to start a new church. And work there was, beginning with fixing some of the places where the water was coming in. We didn't start with the large, flat roof above the hall, but worked on the round tower first. We soon had the place dry. Then we painted and put in a decent floor and floor covering. Soon we were pretty well ready to start meeting there. It was exciting indeed! Several people from Antwerp helped, as did some from in and around Beerse and even farther away.

The inner conviction for a move increased, as did the need, because of all the driving I did to Beerse and Limburg for studies and visitation. Because of the growing interest in Limburg, I already was praying and planning for a church there. We prayed often, alone and with others, and confirmation from others also strengthened our conviction. We read God's Word, and nothing came up that seemed to indicate that we were on the wrong path. The more we read the Word, the greater our inner peace, all the while praying the words of Exodus 33:15: "If Thy presence go not with us, carry us not up hence." We really meant that; it wasn't an easy way of saying, "Oh well, if the Lord doesn't want us to move, He'll stop us." No, it was the constant cry of our hearts. We discussed it time and again with our co-worker and some of the people of the Antwerp church, and they were all in agreement. So the decision was made to move to Beerse after the children finished the school year in June. A lot of work would have to be done to the house part of the mill before we'd be able to move in during July or August; however, there was one real problem.

100. Problem Solved, Thank God. Moved to Windmill in Beerse

Our house in Antwerp was rented with a three-year contract. If we left before the three years were up, we'd have to pay at least three months' rent. That was a real problem for us, as we didn't have much money, and we needed every cent to fix up the house in Beerse. What to do? We prayed about it and talked it over with our co-worker, and he and his wife decided to rent our house. Together we went to see the landlord to talk with him about our move. We told him that we had a couple who would like to rent the house and take over the contract. It took some talking, but after some time he agreed, since we'd been very nice to him and kept the house in good condition. Thank God! What a relief to not have to pay anything. Praise the Lord! It was an answer to prayer, and showed us again that ***God cares and is real.***

We started getting things ready to move. Two youths from our home church in Canada came over towards the end of June. The girls stayed with us for about three months. They were a tremendous help in getting ready for the move. After the move, they scraped off and cleaned the outside walls of the mill and repainted the whole place. What a job! How thankful we were for them. They slept high up in the round tower, going up two narrow stairs to their "bedroom." Other people helped us fix up the house—painting, wallpapering, putting in central heating, and completing other jobs. Finally, the place was ready and we moved in. One of the first services held at the mill was the wedding of a young couple from Beerse, right in our living room. It went really well, but it caused a lot of talk in the town. Sadly, when the wedding and the feast were over and people went home, something very tragic happened.

101. A Sad Experience

Because the wedding took place in the mill and not in the Catholic church, the parents and other family members of the bride did not attend, which was very sad. But the groom's parents and his grandfather were there; the grandfather even remarked on how much he enjoyed the service. After the wedding, as the parents drove the grandfather home, a car from a side street ran a stop sign. They crashed into it, throwing the grandfather from the back seat into the front windshield. They were all taken to a hospital, where the grandfather passed away some time later. We were heartbroken. You can well imagine how this was talked about in the town, some even suggesting that it was God's punishment for not marrying in the Catholic church. How ridiculous! We really sorrowed with the family.

Life went on and so did our little church. We had now started meeting in the round room of the mill. We came together in a very simple way, with a table in the middle on which a loaf of bread and a cup of wine were placed. We'd have a time of singing first, after which the children went to their Sunday school rooms in our house, and the adults continued with readings from scripture, singing, and praying, thus worshipping the Lord. Different ones would participate, and it was wonderful to see and hear these young believers. The service would end with a short message. Teaching was given in Bible studies during the week. I wonder whether the early Christians met like this. We know that in many parts of the world where there is no freedom of religion, Christians still meet in this way—in attics, in basements, in the woods, and in other secret places. We need to be thankful for and make good use of our freedom. Jesus said "I must work the works of Him who sent Me while it is day; the night is coming when no one can work" (John 9:4). How we need to take these words to heart and follow His example!

But then something very strange happened.

102. A Voice

Much work was being done to the mill. Two men from Operation Mobilization (OM) came to help. One of them, Martin Luesink, had been my best man at our wedding. They fixed the large flat roof, and what a job it was! Two young men from Beerse dug a large hole in the hall, which would become the baptism tank and in which hundreds and hundreds of people from all over Flemish Belgium, plus a few of my family members from Holland, would later be baptized. What a job that digging was, as the ground was like clay. A young Christian, who was a mason, came to build the tank. And there was much, much more to do, both inside and outside. Work during the day and Bible studies and visitation at night. And then I had this strange experience.

One night while driving through a wooded area to Limburg, I heard a voice come from the back of my Volkswagen bus, saying "You need to move again." I was shocked! Whether it was a real voice or just something in my head, I'm not sure. I'm very careful with these things, but it was so real that I looked back to see where the voice came from. When I got home late that night, I told Marina about this, and she said that she'd also felt that day that we needed to move again. This was ridiculous ... we had just moved, and now again? I argued with the Lord and told Him we couldn't do this, but the strong impression continued and wouldn't leave us. As the inner conviction grew, so also did the need in Limburg. The Bible studies increased, people were converted, and we transported quite a number to be baptized in a church in Brussels. A local church needed to be planted, but who could do that? I told the Lord that we wanted to be absolutely sure He was prompting us. If this really was from Him, He would have to provide a house and a meeting place for us in Limburg. I would not look for anything myself. And then, some time later, we received a phone call.

103. Yes, This Phone Call

Our three daughters were attending a Catholic school in Beerse. They rode there on the bikes we'd bought them and with which they were so happy. Their teachers were nuns. Our youngest one, Renee, was six years old. She came home one day a bit upset, because the nun had told her that babies should be baptized, and Renee hadn't been. I told her to take her Bible to school and ask her teacher to show her where it says that babies should be baptized. She came home that afternoon with a smile on her face. "The nun couldn't find it in the Bible," she said. Some time later, she came home saying that the nun had told her that children who were six years old should do their first communion. Again I told her to take her Bible to the teacher. When she came home I asked her about it, and again she told us that the nun had not been able to find it in the Bible. It was a good lesson for our young daughter.

And then we received this phone call. It was from Leen in Limburg—the lady who had accepted the Lord the night I was with her and her husband and their friends. She and some others knew about our thoughts of maybe moving to Limburg. "Richard," she said, "you need to come. We've found a house for you."

We were very surprised, as we'd told the Lord that He would have to find us a place; we would not look for it ourselves. We drove to Limburg, and Leen took us to Koersel, a town not far from where she lived. She introduced us to the brother of the owner, who showed us the place that was for rent. It was a large house with a big living room, which would be good for Bible studies. Behind the house was a large garage, and built onto that was a large hall that had been used as a sewing workshop. It was just perfect; we couldn't have found a better place. But then we heard who the owner was.

104. "Visiting" a Prostitute, and Canada

To our great surprise, we were told that the owner was a prostitute in Antwerp who ran the "Blue Room." I had to go and see her, but I didn't want to go alone. Just imagine some young Christian seeing me going into that place ☺! I asked my co-worker to go along. We had a very nice conversation, and there was no problem renting the house. In fact, she promised to come to the official opening, which she did some months later. She came with one of "her men," and even brought a large plant as a gift. I'm fast-forwarding a bit now. We had a wonderful opening service, and I really preached the gospel, clear and plain. Someone sitting in front of her heard the man say to her, "Quite the change … from a whorehouse to a church." The woman's brother lived close by, and anytime there was something we needed, we'd go to him. We had a good relationship.

We sought the Lord for guidance and decided to move at the beginning of 1975 during the Christmas holidays. Martin Luesink and his wife, Marjorie, were working with OM in Belgium. After much prayer, they decided to move into the mill in Beerse and take over the work there. Realizing that once we had moved to Koersel it would be difficult to go on furlough, Marina and I decided to take a five-week trip to Canada to visit Marina's relatives, as well as our home church and other churches and friends who had been supporting us. We had a number of meetings in churches in southern Ontario. Two wonderful men from our home church rented a car for us to drive West and stop in at churches along the way. The first stop was in Sault Ste. Marie, about 740 kilometres from where we were. A meeting was planned for the evening, but as we were nearing the city, driving eighty kilometres an hour, a car from a side road ran a stop sign, and there was a terrible crash!

105. Divine Intervention and Protection. God Is Real!

Because the side road was sort of hidden, we didn't see the car coming until he was pretty well in front of us. I slammed on the brakes as we hit the car right in the middle, causing it to roll over a number of times, ending up on its side in the bushes. We sat somewhere in the middle of the road a bit dazed, still shocked at what had just happened, but mostly surprised that we weren't really hurt. Marina had nothing! I broke my top dentures when I hit the steering wheel with my mouth. I also hit the left side of my chest, which later showed some blue spots, but no broken bones at all. It was absolutely amazing! The policemen shook their heads in utter disbelief. Imagine hitting a car at that speed without safety belts (they weren't in use then in most cars). Marina should have been thrown against the dashboard, but inexplicably, she hadn't been. Was there an angel between her and the dash?

It took some time to free the young driver, who was the only one in the other car. He was seriously hurt and in the hospital for a long time. The police called the people we were going to stay with, and they came to get us. Our car was a total wreck and completely written off. I called Ollie Shantz, one of the men who had rented the car for us (the other being Edgar Martin), and told him what had happened. I glued the two pieces of my dentures together and still preached that evening, but there was a crack between my front teeth. As I spoke, the skin of my top lip would get squeezed, and it really hurt! But the Lord gave grace, and we had a wonderful meeting. But what to do now? We had just started our trip, and now no car!

106. Meetings and Visits in Western Canada

After the meeting, Ollie Shantz phoned and told us that he had another car for us and that he'd be driving through the night to get it to us by morning. The following day, we took my dentures to be repaired. Shortly after we got home, Ollie arrived with a brand-new Ford Crown Victoria; it had only six miles on it when he picked it up. It was a real beauty! After some coffee, we took Ollie to the airport, and that same morning he flew home again. Dear brother! After lunch, we picked up my dentures and started out farther West. That night I was to speak in a church in Thunder Bay, about 700 kilometres from where we were. We had phoned the night before and cancelled the meeting, as we wouldn't be able to be there on time. The next evening, I was to speak in Winnipeg, Manitoba, about 1300 kilometres from where we were.

We drove as far as we could that day, spent a short night at a motel, and drove on to Winnipeg, where we had a wonderful meeting. What a joy to be able to tell folks about what God was doing in Belgium. The next day we drove almost 800 kilometres to Marina's parents' home in the province of Saskatchewan; it was wonderful to see them again after three and a half years. We stayed there a few days while visiting friends and relatives. We held meetings in Regina, Saskatoon, and Moose Jaw, and also in Edmonton, Red Deer, and Calgary in the province of Alberta. What a blessing to find so many folks praying for us. So encouraging! From there we drove back to Marina's parents, and a few days later back to Ontario—almost 3,000 kilometres. We drove through the US, which was faster. We had a last visit with our home church and friends there, after which we flew back to Belgium. We were glad to be home again with our children, who were so happy to see us. What did the Lord have in store for us next?

107. God Providing New Workers

Before we left Canada, we had made one more very important visit. We went to see Hank and Beryl Gelling in Clinton. They had visited us at the beginning of 1974 in Antwerp, and we'd talked and prayed about the possibility of them joining us in the work in Belgium. However, once they were back on the farm, doubt set in as to whether they could be useful in Belgium, and if it was really God's will for them. How could they know? All along Beryl felt they should go, but Hank had doubts. When we visited them this time, we had a good conversation. In the words of Hank, "You told me to get serious with God." After talking and praying together, they decided to come over in the summer of 1975, if the Lord continued to lead that way. And that is what happened. More about that later.

Han and Heleen Stolk, a young couple from Holland, stayed with our children while we were in Canada. Heleen had helped organize the first youth weekend on my uncle and aunt's farm in eastern Holland after our move from Canada. She was very involved in all the youth weekends that followed, and she also stayed with us for several months during the first part of 1974. She would often go along to Beerse to babysit a young boy of a single mother who wanted to attend the Bible study. It didn't take long before she was saved. Han and Heleen were married that summer and I had the privilege of leading the wedding service.

After we returned from our brief time in Canada, I continued with the Bible studies in Beerse and in Limburg, where people were coming to the Lord continually. The need to start a church became urgent. When driving to Limburg, I'd often go during the day to work on the house we'd rented in Koersel. Every room needed wallpaper, paint, and new carpets. There was a lot of work, but I had help from some of the new Christians. Soon we would be in a Limburg, trusting the Lord to start our third church.

108. A New Church

Yes, a third church … and we'd only been in Belgium three years. The church in Antwerp was doing well, as was the much smaller one in Beerse. We sensed the moving of God's Spirit. We didn't have to do any evangelism, like going from door to door or holding campaigns. I'd just begin a home Bible study with a small group. People were totally ignorant of the Bible, as none of them had ever had one, and they were so surprised at what they found. They'd look at me with their eyes, and sometimes their mouths ☺, wide open as I told them that I was sure that I would go to heaven when I died. They'd never heard anyone say that before. Of course, they'd question me about that. "Are you better than us? Have you done so many good works?"

Oh, the joy of then explaining the gospel and telling them that I was no better than anyone else, that I was as big a sinner as they, but that Jesus died and paid for my sin on the cross and called out "It is finished," (John 19:30) it is paid for, the work is done! God said that if we acknowledge our sins and turn to Him and accept what Jesus has done, we will be saved. Again, what a joy to see the startled expressions on their faces; they could hardly believe this, but some did quite soon accept Jesus and experience the new birth. Once this happened, they couldn't keep quiet about it. Their walk and talk changed, which drew the attention of others, who became curious and came along to the study. It was just wonderful to experience the moving of God's Spirit. **How real God is!** We hadn't particularly wanted to go to Belgium; Marina had her eyes on Africa, and I didn't want to go back to crowded Europe, but now we thanked God over and over again for having sent us here to be part of this wonderful work. And this was only the beginning!

109. Moving to Koersel

We're into 1975 now, and we've moved from the mill in Beerse to our house in Koersel, province of Limburg, in east Belgium. Next to this province is another province called Limburg, but it's part of the Netherlands. I went to high school there in the city of Heerlen, and it's from that city that I immigrated to Canada in

Richard Haverkamp

1958. So here we are, and there is excitement in the air for at least four reasons: One, more people are coming to the Lord, especially in Limburg, while the Bible studies keep growing. Two, the large hall at the mill in Beerse is being worked on, but it will take a long time to get it ready for all the baptisms that are going to take place there. Remember the words, *The place will throng with people* (see story #94)? Three, the amazing provisions from the Lord for the work at the mill continued to bless us. Four, two couples are coming to join the work, Martin and Marjorie Luesink, who moved into the mill, and in June, Hank and Beryl Gelling will join us in Limburg.

Living in Koersel, I was able to give more attention to the young believers and Bible studies there. I also continued to go to Beerse a couple of times a week for Bible studies and to help with the work at the mill. Saturdays were especially busy, as a number of young believers would come by to help with the renovations. The large hall had been used to keep chickens, so one can imagine what it looked like. We had to put in sewer pipes, water pipes, drainage pipes, toilets, and a cement floor. The walls had to be redone and a new ceiling put up. A large baptism tank was built with bricks that the owner of the mill, who had a brick factory, donated, for which we were very thankful. We also had to put up light fixtures and other things. And there was much more to be done ... too much to mention. But where was all the money going to come from?

110. God's Provision Again

Looking back now, I still wonder where all the money came from. Because we worked with volunteers, the labour was free—except for meals, coffee, and extras—but all the materials (cement, indoor and outdoor paint, ceiling materials, electrical materials, and water and sewage materials) had to be bought. The money came, some from young believers and some from our co-workers, but most came from Canada as our support went up without us asking for any funds. Absolutely amazing and proof that God was in this. We give Him all the glory! ***And again confirm that God is so real.***

On Sunday mornings, Marina and I and our daughters would drive to Beerse, a forty-five minute drive, for the morning meeting in that town. We'd start with an open session of singing and announcements, after which the children would go to their Sunday school classes. Marina was responsible for this, as Marjorie didn't know the Dutch language yet, but she would also help. The adults would celebrate the Lord's Supper and hear a message. Then we would drive home and get ready for the Bible study in our house in the evening. After a while, we started with a once a month Sunday evening meeting, at which we celebrated the Lord's Supper as in Beerse.

A doctor from Peer attended the first meeting. He was a fine Catholic man, but not a born again Christian. I will call him Philip and his wife, Ingrid. Ingrid couldn't attend, as she was very pregnant. Since I knew he wasn't a real child of God yet, I explained the meaning of the Lord's Table and who could take part. Philip got the message and let the bread and cup pass. I had met Philip and Ingrid some time ago in the fall of 1974. They came to the home of Martin and Lydia Symons, our future Flemish full-time workers. Martin had been asking them for some time to meet with me, but they were hesitant. Now, however, they were ready to come, but they brought two Catholic priests along!

111. An Interesting Meeting with two Priests and a Doctor and His Wife

Well, it became a very interesting evening. The discussion between the two priests and myself was very polite, even though I put one question after another to them, for which they had no real answer. They were familiar with many of the Bible texts I quoted or showed them, but they said that these could not be taken literally. I kept at them until they quite evidently started to become uncomfortable and excused themselves, saying they had another appointment to attend. After they were gone, I asked Philip to read aloud one Bible text after another as answers to the questions I had asked. When they went home, they took the Bibles I had given them. Much later, Ingrid told me that on the way home, Philip had said, "Richard doesn't interest me, but I'm going to read the Bible." I know what he meant; it was not Richard the person who had touched his heart, but the Bible! And that is so good. I often told folks that it wasn't me, or us, who they needed, but God's Word. You don't need to come to us, as long as you go to the Lord and His Word.

I'd noticed their interest and went to visit them a number of times. Ingrid wasn't all that happy with the visits, as she had a stronger bond with the Catholic Church than did Philip. He kept talking to priests, asking them what he needed to do to go to heaven. They would give different answers, but it all came down to the same thing—do your best. One Sunday evening during the winter of 1974, they invited a couple with whom they were friends to come and talk with me. This couple also brought a Catholic priest along, but his answers were quite vague, superficial, and not satisfying to Philip. In time, the biblical answers he received from me began to sprout, and soon something wonderful would happen! I left their house at 2:00 a.m. with joy and anticipation in my heart.

112. No Bibles in a "Christian" country

When we came to Belgium in 1971, we found that people did not have Bibles. In fact, we met people who told us that they weren't allowed to read the Bible, because it was a "Protestant" book. Of course, the church will deny this, but that is how people experienced it. Things have changed, and today children in school are to have a Bible, as our daughters did when they attended a Catholic school. But they are told right away that the Bible is full of myths and mistakes, so how can they trust that book? You should have seen how excited people became when they received a Bible for the first time and began reading it and attending Bible studies where the Bible was taught. Many came to a personal knowledge of the Lord Jesus Christ and were born again. They experienced real forgiveness and received peace. I could tell you story after story, and it proved to me time and again that *God's Word has real power*—power to save and change lives! What a joy we experienced time and again.

113. A Doctor Experiencing and Testifying that God Is Real

Due to our involvement in Beerse, we hadn't yet started a church in Koersel, but we held our first Lord's Supper there on a Sunday evening at the beginning of March. Philip, the doctor from Peer, was present. I had visited him and his wife regularly, and I realized that God was working in their hearts. About two weeks later, two miracles happened as two births took place. The first was that of Philip and Ingrid's second child in the hospital, and the second took place in their home ... in fact, in their bedroom. I'll let Philip tell it in his own words:

"While Ingrid was in the hospital with our second baby, I gave my heart to Jesus in bed one night. Tears of remorse rolled down my cheeks—remorse for all the wrong things I had done, knowing that I would still do some of them. Tears of shame that Jesus, the Son of God, had to die on a cross to pay the debt of my sins, and the sins yet to be committed, with His sacrifice.

But also, and especially, I cried tears of joy—joy because God's grace had befallen me. Joy, not only because Jesus had died for my sins, but had also risen from the dead. He was, and is, the Victor. And I wept because of the joy that Jesus had given me eternal life, and through the truth of His Word, had given me assurance of that. I felt soaked with a warm, unspeakable joy. I was born again; I was a child of God! And because of my new birth, I felt really liberated. Jesus was my Redeemer, my Saviour, and my Lord. He had completed everything for me; He had paid for my sins. I didn't have to perform anymore to be found good enough. Through Jesus, I had become a child of God. I wanted to live for Him."

Wonderful indeed; praise God! And many more wonderful things happened that year.

114. Experiencing the Miracle of the New Birth

I hope you enjoyed reading the shortened version of Philip's testimony. I certainly did. Before sharing some other wonderful things, I want to add a few more sentences from his testimony:

"How was it possible that I had not 'seen' this before? I had a decent Christian upbringing. I'd gone to Mass daily until I was eighteen. Even in Leuven (the university city), I'd gone to church every Sunday. I'd heard passages from the Scriptures read and had read them myself. What was different now? It was God's Spirit who, through my new birth, was working in me."

How true and important these words are. They make me think of Jesus' words: "Except a man be born again, he cannot see the kingdom of God" (John 3:3, KJV). I have many reasons for believing in God, and one of them is the miracle of the new birth. It's wonderful to see how people suddenly "see" or understand spiritual things. I have to think of that one line in that beautiful hymn, "Amazing Grace," which goes like this: "Once I was blind, but now I see." Have your eyes been opened? Are you born again? If not, why not go to Jesus right now and admit your sinfulness in God's eyes and ask Christ to come into your heart? You too will "see" and know exactly what we mean.

Some time later, Ingrid also accepted Jesus into her heart, and the two of them, together with others, were baptized in the mill in Beerse on June 22, 1975. Praise the Lord! Two days before that, on June 20, our new co-workers from Canada, Hank and Beryl Gelling, along with their three children, arrived in Belgium and moved in with us. They came along to Beerse for the morning service and the wonderful and joyful baptism in the afternoon—quite the introduction to God's work in Belgium! On August 15, they moved to a house they had rented in Peer. Guess what that house was later used for?

115. God's Work Growing

Yes, you guessed right—the new church in Peer started meeting there on Sunday mornings towards the end of August 1975. Wonderful! The third church had officially started, praise God. The church grew so rapidly that very soon the Gelling's house became too small, so the church moved to the new house of a kind couple. I'll call them Janine and Geert. I'd previously met with a number of Philip and Ingrid's friends at their house, and had invited these folks to another evening. When I finished speaking, the doctor spoke up. "Because we are living in an old house, with the medical rooms on the main floor and the living quarters upstairs, and a dangerous steep stairway and an unstable wooden floor, I'm afraid of what might happen in case more people show up." Thankfully, Janine spoke up and offered to have the meeting at her new house, so a new weekly Bible study was started there, and now the Sunday services were being held there too.

There were now four Bible studies being held: one in Peer; one a few miles south of Peer in Martin and Lydia's home, which drew quite a number of young people, including some boys from a boys' home; one in Zolder, further south; and one in our house in Koersel. There were now new Christians in at least seven towns in the province of Limburg. In a few years, there would be new churches in several of these towns. The Holy Spirit was moving. Wonderful! Many a night I drove home with tears in my eyes—tears of joy for these dear people, and of joy for being God's instrument in giving them the true gospel. It was heart-warming, but also heartbreaking, to watch the amazement of these folks as they heard the true message of salvation for the first time in their lives, even though they lived in a so-called "Christian" country! ***Now they truly experienced that God is real indeed.***

Towards the end of the year, something very sad happened.

116. God Is Real, but so Is the Enemy, Satan, also Called the Devil

We are in a spiritual battle; the devil, Satan, is real. He's not like some portray him—a figure with horns and hoofs. We understand from the Bible that Satan was once the most important and beautiful angel in heaven (Ezekiel 28:1–19), personified as the king of Tyre. He rebelled against God and was cast out of heaven. Ever since, he's been at war with God, seeking to destroy God's work. He attacked Adam and Eve in the Garden of Eden. Jesus had just been born when Satan sought to use King Herod to destroy Him. After Jesus was baptized, He was led by the Spirit into the wilderness and was there attacked by the devil. When the Holy Spirit came at Pentecost and the church was born, Satan immediately stirred up opposition, and persecution started. As true children of God, we shouldn't be surprised when we are attacked, especially when we seek to do God's work. Satan will often seek to attack the message first, and if that doesn't work, he will seek to get at the messenger.

This is what happened to our co-worker in Antwerp. He started having personal and family problems, which became so serious that he had to leave the work in 1976 and eventually return to

Canada. The young Christians were shocked. How could this happen to someone who had been so used by the Lord? But we need only look into Scripture and see that some very well-known people had personal and family problems. Think of Abraham, Jacob, and especially, King David, whom God called, "a man after my own heart," (Acts 13:22). They were spiritual giants, yet frail human beings. The enemy of our souls attacked them in their weakness and sought to bring them down.

I met with the Lord's people in Antwerp and explained things to them. I spent time with the leaders, and, amazingly, even though a couple of people left, the church kept functioning and is still active, even though it's had its ups and downs, like so many others.

And then we got company!

117. Special Company from Canada

Yes, wonderful company! Towards the end of 1975, Marina's parents came to visit us, which was just great, especially for our children. We took them to see my parents in Holland, as they had met in 1967 when my father and mother had come to Canada for a visit. Having the grandparents look after our children made it possible for Marina and me to get away for a few much-needed days of rest in a quiet place in Holland. We also drove Marina's parents to Switzerland, which was only a day's drive from where we lived in Belgium. We stopped in at friends of Marina's parents, members of the Janz Team, who were holding evangelistic meetings all over Germany while living in the Black Forest area. These people had been members of Marina's grandfather's church in Saskatchewan. What a reunion! But as all good things come to an end, Mom and Dad returned to Canada, and we continued with the work of the Lord in Belgium

A few months later, we had company again—quite important company. Two elders and their wives from our home church in Canada came to visit us. They told us that they'd been sent by our church to check up on us and to see if what I was writing in our monthly letters to the church was true—that more people had become Christians, that we'd had another baptism, or that a new Bible study or even a new church had been started. They had a hard time believing all that, but they soon discovered that it was all true, and they were delighted! We visited our Antwerp church on a Sunday morning. People were really participating in the service, so much so that the elders didn't even get a chance to get up and say something until the end of the meeting. They were quite impressed! They also visited the churches in Beerse and in Peer, and again they were thrilled with what God was doing.

One night I took them to one of my home Bible studies, but as we entered the living room, I was a bit shocked!

118. Different Cultures, Different Customs, Different Convictions

You see, that fairly small room was not only filled with about twenty-five people, but it was also full of smoke, and the table was cluttered with beer bottles and glasses, some of which were still half full. *Oh dear,* I thought, *what are my elders going to think of this?* Forty years ago in Canada, smoking and alcohol were taboo in most evangelical circles, just as in other cultures there are other taboos. For example, we had a Russian preacher visiting Belgium

Richard Haverkamp

several years ago, and he was quite upset that women wore slacks to church meetings.

Some years ago I heard the following story. Members of an evangelical church in Germany had heard about the behaviour of Christian women in America—that they were wearing miniskirts, using lipstick, and wearing earrings. They were quite upset about this and decided to send a delegation to America to investigate, because this was pretty serious. Sure enough, when they came back they called the church together and affirmed what they had heard; in fact, it was even worse. They all became so sad that many started crying, even some of the men. As they cried, their tears ran down their cigars into their beer glasses ☺! Different cultures, different customs, different convictions, right?

We had a wonderful evening as I taught the Word of God, followed by a time of questions and answers. Then we had a brief time of prayer, which we did in some home studies. It was wonderful to hear these new believers, baby Christians, pray. Just short sentences thanking the Lord for the Bible, for Jesus, or for their salvation. After more coffee and discussion, we left the house and got into my car. As we were driving along, I started asking the elders what they thought of the meeting. They were just delighted and happy with what they had seen and heard. Then again very carefully, I asked, "But what about the beer glasses and the smoke?"

119. A New Christian and Her Husband's Reaction

To be honest, I was a bit nervous, as these were the elders of our home church, which was partly supporting us. However, I soon let out a sigh of relief when I saw their smiles and heard them say,

"Oh, Richard, don't worry about that. Give these young believers time. There's no doubt in our minds that we're seeing a genuine work of the Spirit of God here, and we're so happy with that." What encouraging words! Inwardly, I praised the Lord for such spiritual men who recognized a work of God. Some time later they returned to Canada and reported to the church what they had seen and heard. There was much rejoicing and giving of thanks for the great things the Lord was doing in Belgium.

We are still in 1976, and I have to tell you about something that happened in Peer that was sad but at the same time wonderful. Towards the end of 1975, a woman in Peer started coming to the Bible study. I'll call her Miriam. She was married to a man I'll call Robert, who had an important position in one of the largest banks in Belgium. Miriam had cancer and was not well; she paid close attention to the teaching of God's Word, and it didn't take long before she accepted the Lord Jesus into her heart. A bit later, she went to Beerse on a Sunday afternoon to be baptized. What a joy! When she got home, her husband noticed that her hair was wet, so he asked if she'd been swimming. She couldn't lie, so told him the truth. He was shocked. Being a good Catholic, at least in his own eyes, he did not approve of this "new faith" or "new religion," as it was called. She asked if he'd be willing to have me come and explain things to him. He agreed to a visit—"but only this once," he emphasized. On one of the last days of December, I sat in their living room.

120. Talking with a Dying Woman's Husband

We had quite a discussion, which lasted between two and three hours. It was mostly a one-way talk. Robert told me right from the beginning that he was a good Catholic and that his church was the only true church of Christ on earth. I explained to him that when his church first started out with the apostles, it was the true church, but that through the centuries it had changed a lot. Miriam had told me that her husband was willing to have me visit them once, but only once, so I realized that this was probably the only opportunity I'd ever have to talk with him.

For more than two hours, I used the Bible to point out how wrong his church was—wrong in claiming that Peter was the first Pope, as he never was, and wrong to call the Pope "father," as Jesus Himself had said, "Do not call anyone on earth your father; for One is your Father, He who is in heaven" (Matthew 23:9). Of course, Jesus was not talking about our earthly father. I also explained that it was wrong to pray to Mary, as she was a sinner just like us, and it was wrong to believe in purgatory, as it's not found in the Bible. On and on I went, ending by telling him that the Catholic Church was wrong in teaching that we must earn our eternal life, as the Bible says that Jesus has earned it for us on the cross. I then said, "That's why I am so sure that I will go to heaven when I die, while you're not sure at all."

Robert just sat there and listened. What could he say? Much of this was totally new to him. I sensed it was time to go. He looked at me and said, "I have to admit that you have something I don't have, but I don't agree with what's going on here in Peer." And that was it, so I left. Meanwhile, Miriam's condition was deteriorating, and she found it difficult to attend the Bible studies. Robert had been told by a doctor that his wife didn't have long to live, so when Miriam asked him if the Bible studies could be held in their home, what could he say? Some sixth months later, this conversation bore fruit.

121. Meeting in a Dying Woman's Home

Every Wednesday evening, approximately thirty or more people sat in their living room, all with Bibles in their hands or on their knees. Robert attended the studies too, probably out of politeness. As time went on and Miriam got weaker, she was no longer able to sit up. The cancer was in her back, and she wasn't able to attend the Sunday morning services anymore. She again turned to her husband and asked whether the Sunday meetings could be held in their living room, which was quite large. Again, knowing his wife's condition, what could he say?

And so, every Sunday, between thirty and forty adults sat around a table in the middle of their living room, with a loaf of bread and a glass of wine on it. The children would meet for Sunday school elsewhere. There would be singing, reading of scripture, and thanksgiving, after which the bread was broken and passed around, as was the cup. This was followed by a brief message. It was all very simple, but very beautiful. I wondered what went on in Robert's heart and mind.

Because of Miriam's inability to function as mother and housekeeper, the Christians looked after everything, such as making meals for the family, cleaning the house, doing the wash, and so on. They tried to comfort the children, who were in their teenage years, and served Miriam in whatever she needed. Of course, Robert was quite surprised and moved by all this, and his attitude changed.

Marina and I and our children were going to Canada for two and a half months of furlough from June until September. Close to our departure time, I visited Miriam every day, reading the Bible with her, praying, and talking. One day I came into the house and greeted Robert, who was drinking coffee in the kitchen. I walked right into the living room, where Miriam was lying on a bed. After having spent time with her, I returned to the kitchen. Robert, with eyes wide open, asked me, "Well, did she tell you?"

"Tell me what?" I asked.

"That I got born again last night," he answered. "I accepted Jesus into my heart, but I'm not leaving the church."

"That's okay," I said, "you just do what the Lord tells you."

One week later, he told me that he'd left the church. I was really surprised and asked what had caused him to do that. He told me that he'd invited the priest to come over, and he'd asked the priest why he'd never told him, in all the years that he'd been a faithful churchgoer, the good news of the gospel. The priest didn't know what to say, which made Robert so upset that he decided not to go back to that church. Imagine going to the "true" church all these years and never hearing the "true" gospel. Now he had discovered *how real God truly is.*

122. Planning a Funeral with a Dying Woman

Miriam was a tremendous testimony. People from all over came to visit and comfort her, but she did the comforting. The priest came to see her, but instead of him praying for her, she prayed for him. Unbelievable! One day she told me that she wanted to plan her whole funeral with me. She gave me an envelope. I asked what it was, and she said that it contained enough money for an airplane ticket for me in case she died before we returned from Canada. "I want you to lead my funeral and preach the gospel and tell the people that I'm in heaven with Jesus," she said. We looked at each other with tears in our eyes and were very quiet for a few moments as we both realized that once I left for Canada, we'd probably not see each other on earth anymore. It was an emotional moment for both of us.

We started planning her funeral—the songs to be sung and the scriptures to be read. She had already started writing her testimony, which was to be given out as her obituary. She would ask one of the men of our church, who was a carpenter, to make her a very simple wooden coffin, which was to be carried by men from our church from her house to the graveyard. The service would be held in her house, with about a hundred people in the living room and the rest standing in the garden, with loudspeakers outside. As we talked about this, we were both quite moved and excited.

"Oh Miriam," I said, "this is really going to be something. I wish you could be there." She laughed out loud! Startled, I looked at her and she laughed again.

"But Richard," she said, "I *am* going to be there!"

Imagine a seven month old Christian talking like that. Amazing! Doesn't it **show the reality of the living God?** I also laughed, realizing that here was someone ready to meet her Lord and Saviour. Inwardly, I was praising God for this miracle of grace, and thanking Him for allowing me to be a witness to the work of His Spirit. I left the house that day with great joy in my heart, as a fairly young woman was ready to leave this earth, and a husband who had just been born into God's family and kingdom.

A wife losing temporary life, and her husband gaining eternal life! It wasn't much later that we said goodbye and left for Canada. I'll talk about our time there later; let me just continue with this.

123. To Canada and Back for a Funeral

On the first Sunday of September, I was preaching for the last time in our home church in Canada, as we would be returning to Belgium about a week and a half later. While I was speaking, someone walked up to me and handed me a note. I opened it and read these words: "Call Belgium as soon as possible." I knew what this meant and explained to the congregation what was going on. Right after the meeting, we went back to the place where we were staying and I called Belgium. Yes, Miriam had passed into glory. Could I come as quickly as possible?

A flight was booked for Monday evening, and I arrived in Belgium Tuesday morning. I was picked up and we drove straight to Peer, where I met Robert and we hugged each other. He was very positive, as the Lord gave him strength. Everything was planned for the funeral the next day. After talking and praying, I was brought home. Marina and the children would come on their own the following week. I had quite a few things to do to prepare for the next day, such as going over my sermon notes, which I'd been preparing along the way. I went to bed exhausted, as I'd not been able to sleep on the plane the night before. I fell asleep thinking about the funeral service, and the fact that most people would be standing outside. The next morning I woke up to the sound of rain coming down. It rained almost all the way to Peer.

124. What a Funeral!

Yes, it rained, like a real two or three-day Belgian rain. I cried out to the Lord, "All these people who have to stand outside, Lord. Please, you are the God of Creation, the God of miracles, the God who parted the Red Sea for the Israelites to pass through, the God who stilled the storm on the lake. You are able to do something about this too. This funeral is for your glory." As I came closer to Peer, the rain started letting up, and as I drove into Peer, believe me or not, (there are plenty of witnesses), the clouds parted. I saw some blue sky and sunrays! From that moment until shortly after twelve o'clock, it was beautiful, dry weather with some clouds and sun, while all around Peer it rained. The doctor's wife, Ingrid, remarked later, "This was the greatest miracle of the day."

The service started at 10:00 a.m., with about a hundred people in the living room. The sliding doors were wide open, and many more folks stood outside on the lawn. There was a microphone and loudspeakers, so that even the neighbours across the road could hear what was happening. There was some singing and some scripture readings; even Robert read a text and spoke briefly. Amazing! Then I preached, explaining the gospel and telling the people what Miriam had told me to tell them—that she was now in heaven with Jesus. You could hear a pin drop. We closed the service with prayer, and then a number of the men from our church carried the simple wooden coffin with a white sheet and a green cross on it to the cemetery. Many people followed, and all along the route people stood watching; it was very moving. This was the first time in the history of this very traditional Catholic town that something like this had taken place. One of the Christians overheard someone saying, "Look at that! You'd think a general was being buried." What a testimony! Later some people came to know the Lord because of this funeral. At the grave we read a scripture, thanked God that Miriam was with Him, and asked again for strength and comfort for the family. As we walked to the hall where coffee and sandwiches were being served, we felt the first drops of rain. It rained the rest of that day and the next. A miracle indeed! To God be the glory! *Is God real or not?*

Yes, to God be the glory. And not only that, but the funeral had touched many hearts. I'm thinking of one woman who was very impressed, especially with Robert's posture. Instead of mourning, he was rejoicing in the Lord. She lived in another town, and when she got home she went to tell a friend about this, which later resulted in a home Bible study in that town and, much later, a new church. But more about that another time. We'll first go back to Canada, from where I had come for Miriam's funeral.

125. Furlough in Canada

During the second half of June, we had flown from Luxemburg to Iceland and then to New York, as that was the cheapest way to go at that time. At the airport in New York, Ollie Shantz, the brother who had brought us a new rental car after the first one was wrecked in an accident close to Sault Ste Marie (see story #105), and his wife, Elsie, had come to pick us up. They had driven over 800 kilometres the day before, stayed overnight in a motel, and were now ready to take us to Ontario, where we would stay with dear friends on a farm not far from our home church. There were seven people in the car plus our luggage, but it was a big Chevrolet, so no problem—nice and cozy ☺.

We were now home "on furlough." These days it's called "home assignment," as the word *furlough* gives the idea of a holiday, and these times are no holidays. They involve a lot of travelling to churches, supporters, friends, and family, while staying in different homes and moving around. Most missionaries are glad to get back to their mission field, as there they live a more even-paced life. For many, the mission field becomes more "home" than the "homeland." In fact, many missionary children have identity problems, as ours did. "Are we Canadians or Belgians?" they would ask. Some children have no problem with that, but others do, so we need to pray for them. Besides that, we had a third "home" problem. Was "home" Belgium or Ontario, where our home church and many friends were, or the West, where our girls were born and where Marina's family lived?

126. Workers Together

We had left "home" in Belgium for the time being, and were now "home" in Ontario, where we spent time fellowshipping in our home church, speaking in other churches, and visiting friends. After some time, we started driving towards "home" in Western Canada, stopping in different cities, such as Sault Ste Marie, Thunder Bay, and Winnipeg, to speak in churches. Next we went to Gouldtown, Saskatchewan, to see Marina's parents. We stayed with them for some time and then travelled to Regina, Moose Jaw, and Saskatoon for meetings and to visit friends and relatives. From there we went to Glaslyn, north of North Battleford, where Marina's oldest brother lived, and where we'd held some wonderful Vacation Bible Schools in the past. We left there to go to the province of Alberta, where I spoke in churches in Edmonton, Red Deer, and Calgary. There we also visited relatives and friends.

You may ask if it was really necessary to visit all these churches and people both in Ontario and out West. Oh yes, it was! Don't forget that these were the folks that prayed for us regularly, and from time to time supported us financially. We've never had a salary, but have trusted the Lord to provide for us, and He has, using different people and churches. Some gave regularly, others only once or several times a year. For them, it was wonderful to hear that their prayers had been answered and their dollars been put to good use. Even though it was a busy and tiring time, it was such a joy to meet these people. Without them, we couldn't have done God's work in Belgium; it was real team-work. They were overjoyed to hear what the Lord was doing there, and we were happy to tell stories of lives totally changed through the Word of God. Time and again we quoted Paul's words to the Romans: "For I am not ashamed of the gospel of Christ, for it is the power of God to salvation ..." (Romans 1:16). How true this is. **The gospel of Christ is the most powerful means to change not only the sinful hearts of men, but also society.** They were encouraged and so were we. All praise to God! So far, 1976 had been an eventful year, but there was more to come!

127. Back in Belgium, and a New Bible Study

From Alberta we returned to Marina's parents' farm and stayed there for a brief time. Our girls had a great time with their grandparents, whom they would not be seeing again for several years. We then returned to Southwestern Ontario. Before returning to

Belgium, I went back to the garage where I had earlier bought a Ford for $1,500. We drove it many thousands of kilometres without any problems, although we did put new tires on it. The garage bought the car back for $1,200. Talk about another little miracle! Praise God!

As mentioned in a previous story, I returned to Belgium about a week and a half before our planned return date, to officiate at Miriam's funeral. Marina and our three girls came later, and what a time they had. Because of the long drive to New York, we'd been able to change their tickets so they could fly from Buffalo to New York and then to Belgium. A short while before leaving, our youngest daughter, Renee, was visiting with Dutch friends who had some wooden shoes sitting around. Renee tried them out and fell, spraining her ankle. She had to be in a wheelchair at the airports, but she didn't mind being pushed around. In spite of the pain, she had a ball ☺!

In the spring of 1976, several Bible studies were held in Limburg. One of them in Peer grew so large that we had to split it, so another study was started with a group of people in Overpelt. The work there kept growing, and a few years later a church was started, which is still going and growing. Praise the Lord!

I mentioned in a previous story that a woman who had been at Miriam's funeral went home to a place called Lommel. She immediately drove to see a friend (let's call her Bea) to tell her about the funeral and to inform her that she had invited Robert and me to her home. Bea was very interested and asked whether she could come and meet us. When we were together, the lady of the house told me that she'd already accepted Jesus into her heart. When I heard that, I challenged her to open her home for a weekly Bible study. She agreed wholeheartedly! I was thrilled, because every time we'd start a study in a new town, I could see a new church there in the future! Every Monday night that fall, her living room was full of curious people—relatives, friends, and others she had invited. They all received a Bible. The following week, some would return with little pieces of paper in their Bibles, having marked things they didn't understand, and we would have some very interesting discussions late into the night. We'd go all over the Bible from one text to another, and they were so surprised at what they found in the Scriptures. There was a lot of smoking too, so that when I got home and into bed with my dear wife, she would say, "Bah, you smell" ☺.

128. God at Work—Wonderful

Soon a number of these people accepted the Lord Jesus and became true born again Christians. Again and again I was amazed at the power of God's Word and how it could change minds and lives. We drove to Beerse with carloads of people to be baptized, as these new believers had a real desire to follow and obey the Lord. There was much rejoicing. For the first while, these new Christians went to the church in Peer on Sunday morning to participate in the Lord's Supper, and the children had Sunday school. Later, a church was started in Koersel, and they attended there until the time came to start a work in Lommel. Marina and I helped with the beginnings of this new church. After the Lord's Supper, I would preach while Marina taught the children in a bedroom and sang with them while playing her accordion. What great times those were, and it was wonderful to see these young believers hungry for God's Word and growing in their faith. This was real New Testament Christianity—so simple, yet so beautiful. *This was experiencing that God is really real.*

However, before all this happened, a call came from the other side of Belgium.

129. East Flanders Calling

In 1976, my first Canadian co-worker, with whom I'd started the first church in Antwerp, left the Lord's work and returned to Canada. We had several good years together, and our two families would get together every Wednesday afternoon when the kids didn't have school. We'd play a game and then have good Belgian french fries together. Our girls have great memories of those times.

While I started working eastward from Antwerp and moved away to Beerse, my co-worker went westward and started a Bible study in a town northeast of Ghent in the province of East Flanders. When he left the work, the couple who hosted the home Bible study, I'll call them Luc and An, contacted me and asked if I could come to continue the study. It was a long drive, between an hour and a half to two hours, depending on the traffic. After praying about it, we consented. So during the Fall of 1976, every Friday after school, we made the drive with the children to East Flanders. I'd teach the Bible study, and Marina would take the children into a separate room and use her accordion to sing with them and tell them Bible stories. We'd stay overnight with Luc and An, as the study went late into the night. The children would be in bed by the time we finished the evening.

My co-worker had been so sure of the Lord's leading in regards to that study and a new work in that area that he'd already rented a house in a town close by. Unfortunately, the house had been used by a biker gang, the Hell's Angels, and was now in terrible condition. We were asked if we would be willing to move in and take over the rental contract of that house to start up a new work in the area. A lot of work had to be done to the house, and we weren't sure how we could do that from so far away. Could we leave the work in Limburg? All kinds of questions arose, but we talked with the Gelling's in Peer and made it a matter of prayer, seeking the Lord for His guidance. And then it became clear to us what we were to do.

130. Preparing for Another Move

No, we didn't have a note with directions drop down from heaven; neither did I hear a voice in the back of our car, like the time the Lord showed us to move from Beerse to Koersel in Limburg. I've mentioned before that we usually go by three signposts: what we see in the Word of God, generally and/or specifically; the inward witness of the Spirit; and the circumstances. The Word in general was clear: "Go preach the gospel to everyone," (Mark 15:16) and other such texts. The inner witness of the Spirit was there, urging us to go into new areas to start churches. The circumstances were clear—there was a real need in East Flanders and a call for help. As we continued to pray for the Lord to guide us, we began preparing to move during the Christmas holidays, after having been in Koersel for two years.

Until the move, we continued with our ministry in Limburg. Every Friday we'd drive to East Flanders, have our Bible study, stay overnight, and then spend most of Saturday working on the house. We received help from a number of young Christians, and even some from the Antwerp church came to help. It was amazing how rapidly the house was fixed up, and we also enjoyed good times of fellowship with these young Christians. We'd return to Koersel in time to have a Bible study in our home on Saturday evening, while Marina had a Bible club with the children in another room. On Sunday mornings, we'd drive to either Beerse or Peer for the Lord's Supper and Sunday school. I continued with a number of home Bible studies, and people kept coming and bringing others who had become curious because of the change they saw in the young believers and their enthusiasm for the Word of God.

The day of our move arrived. I got out of bed that morning to get dressed and ready for the truck to come, but then all at once doubt arose ... real doubt. Are we really doing the right thing? Are we really sure this is the will of God? I almost panicked. Have you ever experienced that? It's like a dark, black cloud coming over you. What to do? Who to turn to? Well, there was only one sensible thing to do. I grabbed my Bible and started reading where I'd left off the day before.

131. Moving Right across the Country

I'd been reading the book of Acts, and that morning I came to chapter 16:

"Now when they had gone through Phrygia and the region of Galatia, they were forbidden by the Holy Spirit to preach the word in Asia. After they had come to Mysia, they tried to go into Bithynia, but the Spirit did not permit them" (Acts 16:6–7).

Something caught my attention, so I read it again. The Apostle Paul wanted to preach in Asia, but wasn't allowed by the Holy Spirit. Then he wanted to preach in Bithynia, but the Spirit didn't permit him. Strange and amazing ... here was someone we may easily call "the greatest apostle of all times," and he wasn't sure of the will of God. Twice he wanted to go somewhere, but the Lord stopped him. It really hit me and lifted me—Paul wasn't sure of God's will, but he kept moving, and as he moved, the Spirit guided him.

Wonderful! Gone were my doubts. We'd been praying all along that God would guide us. We felt we were on the right path, and the Lord hadn't stopped us or redirected us, so we would go right on. Much later it became evident that this was indeed the will of God, as many people were saved in East Flanders and later in West Flanders, and seven churches came into being in those two provinces in less than ten years.

So we moved. Praise the Lord—a new adventure with Him! My co-worker, Hank Gelling, went with me to visit the prostitute in "The Blue Room" in Antwerp to ask if the Gelling's could take over the contract before the three-year expiry date. She was very nice and said there was no problem, so after we moved out, the Gelling's moved in, from Peer to Koersel. Even though we'd already held Bible studies in that house, and from time to time had celebrated the Lord's Table there, now, on the third Sunday of January 1977, the official start of the new church in Koersel took place. Praise God. Now there were four churches: Antwerp,

Beerse, Peer, and Koersel. A fifth one would be started soon. All that in five years; the Holy Spirit was moving. Amazing!

132. First Conference Outside of Belgium

Yes, indeed ... amazing, and yes, indeed, it was the moving of God's Spirit ... certainly not our work. We were just the instruments He used at that time, and what a great privilege to be used by Him! It was really something for a European Catholic country to see people converted almost every week, and we saw this happening in East Flanders too. We moved to a town called Lovendegem, about a twenty-minute drive northeast of Ghent. The Bible study at Luc and An's place was moved to our house. Those attending had friends and relatives who became interested, so I visited some of them in their homes. Several started coming to the Friday evening study, and conversions took place at a rapid pace. By the summer, we had some sixty adults and children in our living room. After singing together, Marina would take the children to another room and teach them while I would lead the Bible study.

The Word of God's blessing spread, and I was asked by OM (Operation Mobilization) to speak at a workers conference in France, in the Château de St. Albain (close to Macon). The other speaker was a wonderful servant of God, Ralph Shallis, who died in May 1995. He had been a missionary and lecturer in North Africa and France. We had a great time encouraging the workers, some of whom were quite discouraged, as France, like other European Catholic countries, is very difficult and not open to the gospel. They wanted to know what we did to see such conversions and such church growth. They asked what our "secret" was. Of course, we didn't have any "secret," just a lot of prayer, enthusiasm, love for the people, and home Bible studies where we preached and taught the Word of God. People became convinced ***that God is real***, and their lives changed. It would take an epistle to explain everything, and I may come back to this later.

I believe many of these dear folks went home encouraged, ready to put into practice what they had heard. There would be many more conferences like this, and I would be back in France at least ten more times in the years to come. Later that year I'd be going to Sweden, but now it was back to Belgium, where exciting things were happening!

133. Accept or Reject

Yes, back to Lovendegem, where people kept coming. New ones came as relatives witnessed to them. I was able to go to the home of Guido and Marianne Dekegel (real names) on a Wednesday evening in April 1977, after Marianne's mother had become a true born again Christian and kept asking her daughter and son-in-law to invite me for a visit with them. They finally agreed, and we had a wonderful evening together. Guido had been to two Catholic boarding schools, and the very negative religious experiences there had turned him off God. However, I explained the Bible and the true gospel to them, and they both accepted the Lord after I left the house. No one knew at that time that in the future Guido would become a wonderful full-time worker, which is why I can use their real names. Not all who were contacted, visited, or came to the study became Christians. One elderly neighbour lady came to a Friday night study. She was, in the eyes of many, "Lovendegem's newspaper," as she always seemed to know everything about everybody, and made sure that everybody else got to know it. I was going through Romans 1 and 2, and when I was finished, she called out spontaneously, "That's the truth, mister; that is really the truth. I'm coming back next week and bringing my friends along." However, she never came again! She hadn't been living a very moral life, and now she was faced with the truth. She realized that she either had to change her ways or reject the truth, which she did. How sad! There is no in-between—we accept the truth, we accept Jesus, or we reject Him; there is no middle ground. As Jesus Himself said, "He who is not with Me is against Me" (Matthew 12:30). Guido and Marianne heard the truth and accepted it; this dear lady heard it too but rejected it. What are you doing with the truth? What are you doing with Jesus?

134. Amazing!

Quite a number of the new believers had come along with me to Beerse to be baptized, and great was the joy! Thus we felt the time had come to start a church in Lovendegem. What is a church? A group of born-again believers who come together on a regular basis to celebrate the Lord's death and resurrection, to study the Word, to pray, and to spread the Good News. We started meeting on Sunday mornings, still in our house, and we'd sing, "break bread," preach the Word, and have Sunday school. By now there were three classes of children. Marina taught one, one of our daughters, Lily, taught another, and a couple of young converts taught the third class, after Marina helped them during the week to prepare a lesson. It was interesting to see that those who started teaching grew faster spiritually than those just sitting in the meetings and listening.

You'll have to pardon me if I repeat some things, but I've just been amazed again and again at God's work in the hearts and lives of people everywhere—in Antwerp, Beerse, Limburg, and now in East Flanders. I'm amazed at the miracle of the new birth, of which Jesus said, "Except a man be born again, he cannot see the kingdom of God" (John 3:3). By "see," He means, of course, "understand." We use that word too when we explain something to someone, as we will often end by saying "You see? You understand? You get it?" Well, I have seen so many people "get it;" *it is so real.* I've often seen the expression on their faces change when the light dawned. It's the same for all kinds of people, from all kinds of background, age, level of education, colour ... you name it. Absolutely amazing! ***God is real. The Gospel is real. The Holy Spirit is real, and so is the new birth!*** Many a time people have told me that they don't understand God or the Bible. I've told them that they're proving what Jesus and the Bible say. You can't understand until you are born again, and that happens when you're willing to admit that you have sinned, and then accept Jesus into your heart. Have you done that? Are you born again? Are your family members born again? What about your neighbours? Maybe you should share some of these stories with them.

135. "Together" Times

There is always joy when a new baby is born. We had lots of joy as we saw so many spiritual babies born all over Flemish Belgium.

Wonderful! There's also joy seeing these babies grow and become spiritual adults, and even leaders. Since once again our living room was getting to be too small, we started looking for a building to meet in, but that wasn't easy. There was nothing suitable in Lovendegem, so we started looking in towns around us. We finally found a building in the city of Eeklo, about thirteen kilometres north of Lovendegem. It had a population of 25,000, but no evangelical church, as is the case with most cities and towns in Belgium. Eeklo was also the town where, a few years later, our three girls would go to a Catholic high school with about 3,000 students.

In time the church moved to an old rented store that we'd fixed up in Eeklo. The large room on the main floor was the meeting room, and the living quarters upstairs were used for Sunday school classes. One of the teachers was our youngest daughter Renee who taught the class with the little ones. We had a few people come from Ghent and also from Maldegem, a town west of Eeklo. Eventually Bible studies and new churches were started in these places.

Although we were busy in our area, I kept going back to Limburg several times a week to teach Bible studies and visit people. I helped in Beerse from time to time as well. But there were also other activities going on. It's impossible to talk about everything that happened, but let me mention a few. For four or five years we held a church picnic on Ascension Day in a large park just east of Beerse. Those were wonderful times, as we had from 150 to 300 people in attendance. We had lots of games, and some people just sat around and talked. We ate together, and later in the afternoon there was singing, with Marina playing her accordion and a number of people playing guitar. The day was ended by either Hank or me giving a brief message. These were great times of keeping in touch with each other and fellowshipping together. They were discontinued when churches started having their own picnics. And then there were the camps and the conferences …

Picnic with many young believers.

The God Who is Real

Camping with children and youth.

136. Camps, Conferences, and a Name

Marina has always had a passion for children. In Canada, she was Child Evangelism Director in southwest Saskatchewan. She held Bible clubs in different towns and taught others to do the same. In Belgium, she organized the Sunday schools of some of the new churches, teaching and also training others to teach. Of course, a camp had to be started, and we soon did this after getting established in Belgium. We began with a one-week summer camp for children and youth. When we left Belgium in 2009, it had grown to three camps for children, two for younger youth, and one for older youth. In Belgium, there were no nice lakefront camping places with cabins like in Canada, so we continually had to look for places. We used all kinds of buildings and/or tents. We held camps in many different places ... too many to name them all ... but through the years they were used of God, and many children and youth came to know the Lord there or experience a fresh touch from God.

I've always been a proponent of conferences, and so is the Lord, I believe. Look at all the Jewish feasts in the Bible ... times when God's people would get together. We gathered the young Christians together at our baptism services and at picnics, and then we started convening conferences, usually using the Belgium Bible College building in Heverlee. We held Sunday school and women's conferences, as well as men's days, and the greatly blessed family conferences. These times were real feasts.

One of the conferences caused us to choose a name for our churches. From the beginning, we did not want a name. We didn't want to become another denomination, but one Saturday we came to the college for a one-day conference. At the same time, the BGM (Belgium Gospel Mission) was also holding a special day. There was a sign with an arrow pointing to the right with the words "BGM Meeting." There was another sign pointing to the left that said, "Haverkamp Churches Conference." That did it. I was not at all happy with that name, so after prayer and discussion, we decided to call our assemblies Evangelische Christengemeenten Vlaanderen (ECV, Evangelical Churches of Flanders).

And then there was a conference in Switzerland ...

137. A Christian Workers Conference

Yes, an invitation had come from International Teams to speak in August 1977 at their European Workers Conference in Switzerland, which was only a day's drive away. It was a wonderful time indeed, and we met some great people. Les and Sharon Frey from our home church in Canada were there as part of a team working in Spain. I had married them years earlier. We also met Joe and Lois Black from the US, who were engaged in the Lord's work on the island of Sicily.

At the end of the conference, a few of us began talking about having a workers conference on a regular basis. Joe and I decided that he would organize it, and I would do the speaking ... at least for the first few years. Marina would get things organized for the children. And so the Christian Workers Conference for English speaking missionaries in Europe was started. From then on we met every year at the end of August for one week. Usually we came together somewhere in France, but we were in Germany at least once. Almost every year more people attended, and once there were about 175 adults and children, but the numbers would go up and down due to people being ill or on furlough. They were encouraging and blessed times, really refreshing for both the missionaries and the children. Often while driving home after the conference our children would be crying, as they missed their new friends so much. This yearly conference is still ongoing.

Back to Belgium now, where things were really moving. I started a home Bible study in Ghent, which grew into a small assembly in 1978. It is still going today, 2017, but is much larger, and now has its own building. But more about this later, for much has happened in Ghent.

A Bible study was also started in Maldegem, in the swimming pool. Not in the water, of course ☺, but in a separate room. This was really something unheard of—a man preaching from the Bible in a swimming pool. It caused some to come just out of curiosity. A little later we moved into the living room of a young couple, whom I'll call Gerard and Griet. They soon became born again believers, as did a few of their relatives and friends. One night a professor from a Catholic seminary attended, see #65. What a shock his words were for the group of Catholic people there!

138. Shocked People, Me Included!

After I'd concluded the Bible study and answered some questions, I asked the professor for his opinion of the Bible. You can read his answer in story #65. I also asked him if he would go to heaven when he died. He said "no," and explained that nobody could know that. I told him that I did, and that I was sure I would go to heaven. I had everyone look up 1 John 5:12–13: "He who has the Son has life; he who does not have the Son of God does not have life. These things I have written to you who believe in the name of the Son of God, that you may know that you have eternal life …" The Catholic people present were so shocked that one of their seminary professors, who would later become a bishop, didn't know if he would go to heaven.

Over the years, I've talked to at least fifty-five Catholic priests in Belgium, and not one of them was sure he would go to heaven—except one, an abbot (head of a monastery). He told me that he had sacrificed so much for God that he would go to heaven for sure. "I have certainly earned it; if I don't go to heaven, no one will." His own words! How terribly sad. If the leaders don't have assurance, or have the wrong assurance, what of the people they teach and lead? What a mission field!

A woman who was a teacher of religion in a girls' high school invited me to come and speak to the girls of two combined classes. She told me that these girls had no interest in God or the Bible. I spoke for an hour and a half. The interest was so immense that you could have heard a pin drop. Afterwards, she took me to a restaurant for coffee and to talk. She was dumbfounded and asked me how I created such an interest. We started talking about the Bible, and at a certain point I quoted Jesus' words in John 14:6, "I am the way, the truth and the life." Her reply? "Who says Jesus said that?" I was dumbfounded!

139. Meeting Unbelief and Experiencing the Power of God

Yes, I was dumbfounded indeed, so I asked her to repeat what she had just said.

"Who says Jesus said those words?"

To be honest, I became a bit irritated and answered, "But it says that clear and plain in John 14."

"Oh yes," she replied, "but our college professor told us that Jesus' disciples saw Him as the way, the truth, and the life, and when they wrote the gospels, they put those words in His mouth, as though He had said them, but we don't really know whether He did or not."

I was quiet for a moment and then said, "But what then did Jesus say and not say?"

"We don't know," she answered.

"Well, who does know?" I replied.

"The theologians" she answered.

"It's hard to find two theologians who agree," I answered. "No wonder the girls you teach aren't interested in what you tell them. Jesus says in Matthew 15:6b, 'You have made the commandment [Word] of God of no effect [powerless] by your tradition.' In other words, according to you, we could all have our own Bible and each pick and choose what we want." That ended the conversation! Dear reader, maybe Catholics reason differently in the country where you live, but this is the way it is in Europe, aside from a few exceptions. This is what is taught in the schools, and this is what we were up against.

The Word of God has power—real power! It isn't just given for information, but for *transformation*! It is meant to change the lives of people. Physical healings are miracles, but the greatest miracle is the power of the Word of God to change character. That's what's most needed in this world. We need something to transform people's hearts from being selfish to unselfish. I wish I could tell you about the people I saw who were changed by the Word of God. I would love to tell you about all the changed lives of alcohol and drugs addicts, and people from broken marriages, but there are too many to mention here. That's what it's all about, and all because of the gospel and a personal relationship with God. That's why I continue to be really excited about the gospel, for it is the power of God to salvation for everyone who believes (Romans 1:16–17). We saw many people believe, not only in our area, but in other parts of Belgium too. Wonderful! Much was happening! ***May I say it again? God is real indeed.***

140. A Special Time

For a period of about twenty years, from the early 1970s to the early 1990s, we had an "open door" in Belgium. People were confused and didn't know what to believe anymore. When a seminary professor who later became a bishop didn't know if he was going to heaven when he died, and when religious teachers were telling the children in school that the Bible wasn't trustworthy and was full of scientific nonsense and historical mistakes, what were they to believe? When our three daughters were taught in a very Catholic school that Jesus didn't really rise from the grave, because "that just isn't possible," what can one expect? This gave us a tremendous opportunity to preach the Bible as the true Word of God and to present the real gospel as the unchanged good news message from God. When people believed and their lives changed, others became interested and started attending our Bible studies. Over a period of twenty years, twenty-four churches were started. There were actually a few more, but after a while a couple of small ones merged, and a couple of small assemblies among the Belgian soldiers stationed in Germany discontinued when the soldiers were withdrawn from that country.

Eventually, that special period of blessing and growth stopped—a period in which people became born again Christians every week, or at times every day. Why did it stop? No one knows. Throughout church history, we see that at certain times and/or in certain places or areas, God performs a special work. And so He did in Belgium, and we were privileged to be part of it. At the same time, I believe our method of evangelism and church planting had something to do with it too. We didn't do much traditional evangelism, like door to door visitation, open air meetings, or campaigns. We found that the best place to evangelize during that time was in people's living rooms. That's where we had our Bible studies, and that's also where a number of churches were started, much like in New Testament times. Notice the phrase, "the church in their house" in the apostle Paul's epistles. Maybe we ought to get back to that; as time goes on, we may be forced into home churches due to persecution, which is already happening in many parts of the world. Are we preparing for that?

141. God at Work, Two New Churches

Yes, that living room evangelism really worked. People who were not willing to come to a tent meeting right in the town square, or stand listening at an open-air meeting where everyone could see them, had no problem coming to someone's living room. We'd often start with a small group, but it would soon grow and become so large that we had to split and start another study somewhere else. That's also the way it went, at least in the beginning, with church planting. Let me use our home in Lovendegem, East Flanders, as an example.

We started with a Bible study, which grew into a church in our home. As more and more people were added to the church, our house became too small, so we moved to a building in Eeklo.

Since a number of people from Ghent were coming to Eeklo, I started a Bible study in Ghent. Soon we had enough new Christians to start a church in someone's living room in that city. When that group grew, we had to rent a building. At the same time, the church in Eeklo continued to grow, and I started a Bible study with a number of people from Maldegem. That study grew, and the people who became Christians came to Eeklo for the Sunday morning service. After some time, a group "hived off", and a new church was started in Maldegem. Our Sunday meeting was very simple: singing, Sunday school, and a communion service, which we called the Lord's Supper, or the "breaking of bread." Different ones would take part, and after the bread and cup had been passed around, someone would give a brief message. Because we didn't need a pastor for every church, as all were encouraged to participate, we were able to start new churches quite rapidly. Teaching was done during the weekly Bible studies.

Most of our churches came into being through a healthy "hive off" from an existing church. Right from the start of a new church, I would tell people that God wanted us to have babies, meaning new Christians, but also new churches. I still believe that. Every church should aim at starting what is sometimes called "daughter" churches. Every church should be a "mother" church. Church planting is the fastest way to evangelize the world, and the world needs to be evangelized. It's in such a mess; only God can change things … when we allow Him to do so. But there has to be a vision for that. Did Jesus not say, "I will build my church?" Are you part of a church with such a vision? If not, talk to your church leaders and encourage them in this. Wonderful things can then happen, as we saw in Limburg.

142. God Adding New Workers

Let's get back to Limburg now, for there were some interesting developments there. As there was real growth in East Flanders, the same was true in Limburg. I still went there quite regularly, and also to Beerse, as our good friends and co-workers, Martin and Marjorie Luesink, felt led to go back to Canada, where Martin looked after Hank Gelling's farm for a year and then moved to Regina, Saskatchewan. Marjorie felt responsible to look after her mother, who was not well. Martin worked for the Canadian Bible College there. They raised five children, of which the older one is now serving the Lord in Greece with her husband. The youngest daughter is a pastor's wife in Alberta. Their leaving Belgium meant extra work for me in Beerse. I will come back to this later.

The Gelling's returned to Canada in 1978 after they'd finished the period of three years to which they had committed themselves. But because the church in Koersel was still quite young and small, the Gelling's, with the blessing of the elders of their assembly, decided to go back to Belgium for another three years. However, by 1980, they realized that they'd be staying in Belgium a lot longer than originally planned, and so they returned to Canada to sell their farm. I remember Hank saying something like this: "What are chickens compared to the eternal souls of people?" In July 1981, they returned to Belgium, and they've been there to this day—June 7, 2017. Praise the Lord! I greatly respect them for making such a sacrifice. We thanked God then and continue to thank Him now for them and their ministry.

As the work in East Flanders grew, so also did the work in Limburg. During this time, another couple, John and Marga den Boer from the Netherlands, who were working with the Belgian Gospel Mission, decided to join forces with us. They were instrumental in starting three small churches, two of which eventually merged so that there are now two still functioning. In 1996, they went back to work with the Belgian Gospel Mission and are still with them today. Until now, the workers had come from outside of Belgium, but now God had something else in mind. Exciting events indeed!

143. The First Flemish Full-time Workers

Let me reintroduce you to Martin and Lydia Symons, the first ones in Peer, Limburg to accept the Lord and be born again (see story #97). They opened their home for Bible studies, and I had many wonderful times with them. A number of people, especially youth, became Christians in their home. After the Peer church started, Martin became one of the leaders. He had a job in a meteorological office and had quite a flexible schedule, so he was able to do a lot of studying. Both he and Lydia were (and still are) very active. Together with another couple, they started a drug rehabilitation program, which would eventually lead to a ministry called Bethesda. This ministry is still active under new leadership.

In 1979, I talked to them about going full-time in the Lord's work, but they weren't ready for that yet. We kept praying for this, and in 1981 they took the step. Martin quit his job and started working full-time for the Lord, trusting Him to supply their needs, as we missionaries were doing. This was a real step of faith, as one can well imagine, and family and friends had their doubts about it. This was really unheard of—to leave a good job and start doing this "religious work" without a salary! But the Lord was faithful and provided for them, even though they had some difficult moments. They're now able to say with the Apostle Paul:

"Not that I speak in regard to need, for I have learned in whatever state I am, to be content. I know how to be abased and I know how to abound. Everywhere and in all things I have learned both to be full and to be hungry, both to abound and to suffer need." (Philippians 4:11–12)

As I said, I have an awful lot of respect for them, and I can't stop thanking the Lord for their faithfulness in the ministry. It's a tremendous joy when people come to know the Lord. It's also a joy to see them grow in the Lord and become mature Christians who take on responsibilities, such as teaching Sunday school or Bible studies, or becoming youth, camp, or church leaders. To see some of them answering the call of God to go full-time into His service is an even greater joy. Martin and Lydia wouldn't be the only Flemish people who would answer God's call. Others would follow; in fact, there are now more Flemish workers than outsiders. Praise the Lord!

But let's go back to East Flanders where amazing things were happening, and also in West Flanders (Flanders Fields). It was the beginning of January, and it was cold in Belgium.

144. Trouble in Our House

We had a sink in our bedroom, but no heating. One morning Marina woke up and heard water running. She discovered that the sink's water pipe had broken because of the frost. The water was running down the wall into our large living room, and the carpet was soaked. Water was also running outside from underneath our front door and forming a layer of ice there … and I was in Texas, US! Marina phoned a friend who came and turned off the water. Then she and our three daughters tried to soak up the water with sheets and towels, but it didn't work. Thank God, several of the new Christians came over for prayer meeting that evening and helped her. They moved all the furniture and hung the rug over a strong rope in our back shed. What a job! When I returned from the States, everything was back in place; thank God for a good wife and willing friends!

You can well understand that with all that was going on, we were busy people—driving to Beerse, Limburg, Eeklo, Maldegem, Ghent and other places; speaking at meetings, holding Bible studies, and visiting folks. We were very happy when the Lord sent others to help. It's a bit difficult to write everything in chronological order, so I'll go back and forth a bit. I mentioned in the previous story that Martin and Lydia Symons went full-time in 1981. Now we go back a bit, because in 1979, the Lord sent a couple with two children from the US to help us in the work. I'd been over there to visit them and discuss everything, and I also spoke in a few churches there.

When Hal and Marion Threadcraft arrived in Belgium, they stayed with us for a little while until they were able to rent a house in Ghentbrugge. They had quite a time adapting, coming from Texas, which is the second largest state in the US, to a little crowded country like Belgium. They also had to learn the language, which isn't easy, but they did well, and soon they were very much involved in the work. More about them later.

But what about West Flanders? Well, I received this phone call from Ingrid, the doctor's wife in Peer ...

145. A Strange Story

Amazing what a short telephone call can bring about! Ingrid called and asked me to visit a couple in West Flanders. The woman, let's call her Christiane, was Ingrid's pen-pal. Once a year she and her husband, let's call him Tony, would go for a weekend to visit Ingrid and Philip in Peer. They had just been there, and the doctor and his wife had talked to them about the Bible. They went home with a Bible under their arm. Now Ingrid called to say that Tony was reading the Bible, and she asked if I could go and visit him and his wife. I said I'd do my best. To be honest, I wasn't happy about this, as I was already so busy, and now I also had to go to West Flanders! It just seemed a bit too much.

I eventually went and was invited in. Christiane made good coffee, which I enjoyed, while Tony told me about his experience reading the Bible. He was eating either a turnip or a carrot, I forget, but with his mouth half full and his West Flanders' dialect, I had a difficult time understanding him, especially as his story just seemed so strange. He told me how he'd started reading the Bible from the beginning and understood that God had given us trees and plants to eat. In fact, in chapter three of Genesis, Eve said that they were allowed to eat from every tree except the tree of knowledge of good and evil. In his garden in the back yard, Tony had some trees and bushes, a couple of which were very poisonous. Since God had said we could eat from every tree, Tony thought he'd try that out, and he ate some of the poisonous stuff. He also gave some to a small pig in the barn. The next day it was dead, but Tony was alright. I didn't quite follow his reasoning, but he was convinced that the Bible was the Word of God. I'll come back to this later.

While driving home from this visit, I told the Lord that I didn't know what to think of this, and that He'd have to look after these folks. Some time later, Ingrid phoned again and asked me to visit them again, as both of them now seemed very interested. With a bit of a heavy heart, I went again, wondering what I was going to hear this time! I could never have guessed what was going to come out of this. Wait until you hear this!

146. A Real Miracle?

When I arrived at Tony's house, the door opened and I received a warm welcome. The coffee was good again, and I enjoyed it. This time Tony wasn't eating anything, so I could understand him much better. We talked about the Bible, and I noticed a tremendous interest. I sensed that God had been working in his heart. The matter of the poisonous trees came up, and he wondered why his little pig had died, while he was okay. I explained to him that when Eve said they were allowed to eat of every tree, except the tree of knowledge of good and evil, she was speaking before the fall, before they sinned, when everything was still "very good." After they rebelled and sinned against God, the whole earth was affected; in fact, Genesis 3 tells us that the earth was cursed and would bring forth thorns and thistles. I told him that there were two possibilities why nothing serious had happened to him: he either had a very strong constitution, or God worked a miracle and protected him. As he'd done this in innocence, and because the Lord still had plans for him, I said that I believed the latter to be true. God had spared him to give him a chance to be saved and to be used of God. Looking at him and listening to him, I wondered whether he wasn't saved already, even though he didn't really know the gospel. I had a wonderful time with Tony and Christiane that afternoon. I get tears in my eyes when I think back to it. Much more would happen yet; within six or seven years there would be five churches in West Flanders and many, many new Christians ... and it all began in this living room. Unbelievable!

147. The Power of a Changed Life

Before I left, I told Tony and Christiane that they needed Bible study, so I offered to come once a week to explain the Bible to them, which they agreed to. But there was one condition: Tony had to invite all his brothers and sisters to come. He was the youngest of a family of eight. He laughed out loud and said that none of them would come. "They're all praying for me to come back to the Catholic church," he said. He didn't go to Mass anymore, and he had quite a reputation. I left with the agreement that the relatives would be invited, and drove home wondering what was going to happen.

When I arrived on the evening of the first study, there were eight people—brothers and sisters and their partners. I was told some time later that they'd come because of the tremendous change in Tony's life. They could hardly believe that he'd changed in such a way, and it aroused their curiosity. **Tony's life demonstrated that God is real.** I introduced myself and gave each one a Bible. For most, if not all of them, this was the first time they'd held a Bible. I took them through part of chapter one of John's Gospel, and then asked whether they had any questions. It was quiet for a bit, and then one of them said, "This is quite something; we've never had the Bible explained this way." One of Tony's brothers-in-law said, "This is against the Catholic Church; you'll never see me again." He didn't come back until some months later, and he's now an elder in one of the churches. Amazing! Ironically, I hadn't said one word about the Church; I hadn't even mentioned it.

We had a bit of a discussion, not too long, as most needed time to digest what they'd heard that evening. I closed with prayer and then made a suggestion. "What if I come for four weeks in a row and teach you the Bible, after which you can decide what to do—either continue, or if you don't agree with what I share, stop, and you'll never see me again." They agreed to have me come for four evenings. I drove home wondering who would be there the next week.

148. Explaining the Gospel in West Flanders, Part of Flanders Fields

When I arrived at Tony's the following week, I was surprised to see that they were all back, except the man who had said he wouldn't be returning. But a few others had come along, which was encouraging. I continued with the study of the Gospel of John, and we had a blessed time. As always, the question arose: "How can you be so sure you're going to heaven when you die? Are you so much better than others? Have you done so many good works?" As always, I smiled inwardly, while at the same time feeling so sorry for these folks who were so religious yet had no assurance at all as to their eternal destiny. What a privilege to explain the true gospel to them and tell them that I was no better than anyone else, and that I hadn't done that many good works to earn a place in heaven. I showed them that Jesus paid my debt on the cross, and that forgiveness and eternal life were gifts from Him. In Ephesians 2:8–9, Paul says that we are saved by grace, which is God's unmerited favour, through faith in what Christ has done on the cross, and that it is not of ourselves, but the gift of God, not of works, lest anyone should boast. No one who enters heaven will be able to say, "I am here because I have done this or that." All will declare, "We are here because Jesus died for us and rose again."

"Yes, but we've always been told that we have to do good works to earn our place in heaven," someone said. I explained that the church had turned things around; it says to do good works and you will (maybe) go to heaven, while the Bible teaches that heaven is God's gift. After we receive His gift, we do good works to show how thankful we are. I sensed that some were really understanding this, so I encouraged them to confess their sinfulness to Jesus and accept Him into their hearts as God's gift.

The four weeks went by quickly, and all were in agreement that we should continue; in fact, that Bible study went on for eight years. Often there were between forty and fifty people present. After three months, this living room became too small, so we had to start a second study in another living room!

149. God's Intervention

A wonderful couple in the ancient city of Ieper (Ypres), right in Flanders Fields, opened their home for this second Bible study. At the end of WWI, there was nothing left of this city, but it was eventually rebuilt. One way to enter it is through a beautiful archway, the "Menin Gate," which has the names of approximately 55,000 fallen soldiers on it. Every night since 1927, at 8:00 p.m., "The Last Post" is sounded. Terrible battles were fought, and there were 1,700,000 casualties[2] (fighting men and uncounted civilians)

The God Who is Real

on both sides in that area. There are close to 150 cemeteries in and around the city, some with only a few graves, and one with 12,000.

Now a different battle was waging, a spiritual one. A number of people from the first study came to this new one and brought friends and family members along. The man who'd said, "you'll never see me again" attended also and both he and his wife became born again Christians. They discovered that **God is real indeed.** It didn't take long before the large living room was filling up. What a time we had! It's impossible to tell everything that happened there, but one incident comes to mind, as it really shows God's intervention.

The study was held on Sunday evenings, but one night I wasn't able to be there due to some other engagement. I asked a dear brother from another assembly to lead the Bible study. I mentioned to him that there would be some new people present, so to make sure not to mention baptism, as it could turn them off. Well, the brother came and led the study, focusing on Joshua crossing the river Jordan. A river has water, and sure enough, he gave quite an explanation about baptism. I don't know why he did this or how he could have forgotten what I'd told him. The lady of the house, who had invited the new people, sat with her head down, praying and wondering how the new ones would react. Nothing was said that evening, but a few days later she saw those people and carefully asked them about the study. They thought it was really good. Very carefully she asked what they thought about what was said about baptism. They looked at her with a blank look on their faces. It turned out that they'd not heard that part. Amazing! The Lord must have closed their ears! Yes, God Himself was at work. Just wait ... there's more to come. Looking back, I thank God that we were allowed to be part of His wonderful work. ***He is so real!***

150. New Bible Studies and New Christians

There was real progress being made. New home Bible studies were started; I hardly knew where to go first or last. The man who had said, "you'll never see me again," opened up his home for a study. Amazing, isn't it? One night some twenty people sat at the large table as this man's brother attended for the first time. As he sat down, I put a Bible in front of him on the table. He moved his chair back as though I'd put something dangerous there. He pulled up to the table again, looked at the Bible, picked it up, turned it around in his hands, looked at all sides of it, and said, "Is this Bible the real one, because there are many Bibles, aren't there? Isn't this something? This is the first time in my life that I've seen a Bible." Unbelievable! Here was a fine gentleman around thirty-five years old, living in a "Christian" country, having gone to church all his life, yet he'd never seen a Bible. How is it possible? He soon became a Christian and a leader in the church. Amazing! ***Is God real?***

I usually led a study of at least an hour and a half in length, after which we had coffee and question time. What does the Bible say about the Pope? Is he really infallible? What about praying to mother Mary and to the saints? What about purgatory? What about the Mass? And so on it went, like having another Bible study. We would go from one text to another, and they were often so amazed at what the Bible taught. This would go on until 12:00 or even 1:00 a.m. Some would go home earlier, but others would stay and ask questions. What exciting times indeed! Many became true born again Christians. On a Sunday afternoon, we'd all go to Beerse to have a baptism service. One couple knew they should get baptized, but were hesitant. They took their camper and drove south to France for a camping weekend, but the camper broke down. They returned home and were baptized the next day, praise the Lord. God's Spirit was moving, and every week some were saved. The words of Psalm 118:23 come to mind, "This was the Lord's doing; it is marvelous in our eyes." But there were problems too!

151. Problems in Spite of God Being Real

Of course, there were problems. One can't have babies without dirty diapers, and we had a lot of babies— "baby" Christians. The Lord had saved them, and they were now on their way to heaven, but God had more in mind than that alone. In Romans 8:29, Paul says that we are predestined to be conformed to the image of His Son. In other words, God wants to make a little "Jesus" out of us. Can you imagine what a world full of little "Jesusus" would be like? Man was originally created in God's image, but that image was messed up because of sin, so God sent a new image of Himself, His Son. He died for us and paid for our sins, was buried and then rose again, so as to be able to give us new life through His Holy Spirit. The Holy Spirit now works in us to make us like Christ, but this is a lifelong process and is not so simple.

People became Christians ... wonderful! But now things needed to change in their lives, and that can be painful and difficult at times. It's one thing to see someone become a Christian, but it's quite another to see this person live like Christ as a true disciple. All parents know that it's one thing to have a new baby, but it's quite another to raise that child to maturity. In the case of discipleship, there was a lot of teaching and counselling involved, but it was wonderful to see people grow in their faith and change to become true disciples.

One of the instruments God uses to refine us is the church. When we become born again Christians, we become part of the universal church of Christ, but God also wants us to be part of a local assembly or local church. Notice how often the church is mentioned in the New Testament. Hebrews 10 speaks of "not forsaking the assembling of each other." Every born again Christian is like a rough diamond, but just as diamonds need to be cut, so also do Christians. God puts us together in the church, and our rough sides rub against each other. This can produce heat. Sometimes it gets too hot, and the Christian says, "I'm not coming anymore; I can believe on my own." But that's running away from God's refining process, and that's too bad, because He wants to make beautiful diamonds out of us! But there was another reason why we had problems.

152. Personal Struggles

When God created the world and mankind, His enemy, Satan, appeared and attacked almost immediately. Within a short time of Jesus' birth, Satan, using King Herod, tried to kill Him. When Jesus wanted to start His ministry, He was led by the Holy Spirit into the wilderness and was there attacked by the devil. Over the next few years, Jesus was constantly under attack. When the Holy

Spirit came on the day of Pentecost and the church was born, Satan came and stirred up opposition, and persecution of the new believers began.

The Christian life is a battle, not a Sunday school picnic. It is warfare. When I accepted Jesus, I became very conscious and aware of the presence of God, but I also became aware of another presence—an evil one. God is real, but so is the devil, and anyone standing up for God will experience that. That's one reason why we have problems, and in a sense, that's a good sign, because it means he's afraid of us and of what we're doing. I've often said that the only place where there are no problems is at the cemetery, but there they are all dead. If the devil never bothers you, you may well wonder if you have any life.

Wherever God is at work, there will be opposition and problems. God was at work in Belgium, and we experienced opposition in many different ways. The enemy attacked our spiritual life, our health, our marriage, our family, our ministry, and so on. All kinds of things happened. Some people who seemed so genuinely converted left us and turned their backs on us, which was heart-rending. There were problems between believers, which is not abnormal, but not easy. There were problems with leaders in the church. We experienced a church split in one area, but thank God, some time later these dear folks met, confessed things to each other, and reconciled. But it took a lot of time and energy, and it was very tiring at times.

A couple of times I became so overwhelmed with the problems that I told my wife, "Honey, pack the suitcase; we're going back to Canada. I'm so tired, I can't take anymore." But fifteen minutes later I'd turn around and tell her to unpack, because we just couldn't leave, not as long as the Lord, who had called us, had not given the word. From then on whenever I'd tell her to pack the suitcase, she'd just wait fifteen minutes before starting! ☺. Yes, it was a real battle, but God was with us, and it was indeed really worth it. You'll see!

153. God's Blessing Being Real

By 1982, we'd been working in Belgium for ten years and much had happened, which made the battle worthwhile. Hundreds upon hundreds of people had been saved, baptized, and brought into local churches. There was an assembly in Antwerp, one in Beerse, and eight in the province of Limburg. Amazing! We also had three churches in East Flanders and three in West Flanders, for a total of sixteen. All praise to the Lord! As far as workers were concerned, the Gelling's had joined us in 1975, the den Boer's in 1979, the Threadcraft's in December 1979, and Martin and Lydia Symons in 1981. In January 1980, a young woman, Joanna Groen, came to work with us in Ghent. She went back to Canada and got married to her boyfriend, Pete Gifford, in June 1981. They came to Belgium as missionaries in May 1985. More about them later.

Besides evangelism and Bible teaching, we started churches and began training leaders. We also held conferences and camps for children and youth during the summer. There was lots of activity going on, and the Holy Spirit was moving, which is really amazing for a difficult West European, Roman Catholic country. Word of the Lord's blessing got around, and I was invited to come and speak at conferences in other countries. During this period, I travelled to Sweden, France, Germany, Scotland, Ireland, Northern

Ireland, Spain, Italy, Austria, and Switzerland. Everywhere we went the Lord blessed the ministry, missionaries and church workers were encouraged. I returned to most of the countries at a later date for more conferences. It was so uplifting to see discouraged missionaries and workers getting enthused again. Yes, it was worth the battle. All the messages were taped, and I heard of one instance in which a worker somewhere in southern Germany got a hold of the tapes, listened to them some twenty times, and started putting into practice what I'd taught. The last I heard, he now has a church with 175 members, praise the Lord! **God is real in Germany too!**

While I was gone, Marina held down the fort, looking after the wellbeing of our children, helping with their schoolwork, answering the phone, and counselling and praying with people over the phone. She taught Sunday school and trained others for that; she had her hands full, but it was worth it. It was such a blessing to see young believers become active and teach and help. But the enemy didn't sit still either, and difficulties arose in our church in Beerse!

154. Struggles and Victory

That difficulties arose in the small church in Beerse was, in a way, not strange. Look at the New Testament churches. Paul writes to the Galatians, "I marvel that you are turning away so soon from Him who called you in the grace of Christ, to a different gospel" (Galatians 1:6). "So soon!" Yes, wrong teaching was coming in already. That's one problem that arises, but of course, there are others. One of the most common difficulties concerns relationships. This is also the greatest problem in the world ... from fights to marriage problems to family feuds to outright wars. Jesus came to restore relationships, first of all between God and men, and then between people, but that doesn't happen automatically, and it takes effort.

There was no false doctrine coming into the church in Beerse, but there was some friction between some believers. Others were having marriage problems, and some were becoming lukewarm. There was also a lack of leadership. All of this together caused a decline in attendance. As it already was a small church, this was disappointing. One Sunday morning when I arrived there, I found only five people at the meeting. This was indeed very sad and discouraging. Some friends thought I was wasting my time and suggested closing the place and letting the Christians go to another church in the next town. I drove home and went to my study, took my Bible, and got down on my knees with the Bible open before me at Matthew 16. I started praying and reading the words of Jesus in verse 18: "... I will build My church, and the gates of Hades [hell] shall not prevail against it."

"Lord Jesus," I prayed, "these are your words. You said that You would build your church. You said that the gates of hell would not prevail against it, but Lord Jesus, in Beerse the gates of hell are prevailing. Are You going to allow that? I will visit people, I will preach and teach, but You must build your church." I prayed like this for quite some time. Today, there is a church in Beerse of approximately forty-five people, which isn't bad for a European Catholic country. They have their own building, and two elders are leading the church. Evangelism is taking place, and last year several people were baptized, praise the Lord. In 1997, the Henry Heikoop family came from Canada to Beerse and lived and worked there for three years. They were a great help in many ways and had a wonderful testimony in the town. I wrote this to show that there is a battle going on, that there is an enemy, but that at the same time, there is a way to beat him. It's by prayer and standing on the Word of God.

Our home was often a busy place. Three churches were started in our living room, and Mom and Dad were pretty involved, which wasn't always so easy for our children.

155. Struggles of Being a Missionary Family

Moving several times was difficult for our children, because of the change of schools, surroundings, and friends. Whenever a new church started in our home, the girls would have to get up in time on Sunday morning to clean their rooms and make their beds, because the rooms were used for Sunday school. Mom was on the phone quite a bit, and Dad was away a lot. Many an evening when I left home to visit or give a Bible study somewhere I would thank the Lord that He had given me girls and not boys, because if I'd had boys, I would have had to stay home to play ball with them … but girls were the mother's responsibility. That, of course, was totally wrong thinking. I realize that now, but not at that time. I understand now that girls need their father just as much as their mother. That's not the only mistake I made as a father. I've apologized to our daughters. One day when I was talking to one of them I said that I was so sorry, that I'd made so many mistakes, and that I wished I could do it all over again. She smiled and answered, "Oh Dad, if you had to do it all over, you would make other mistakes." She has three daughters herself and knows that perfect parents don't exist.

Of course, there are positive sides to being a missionary child, such as learning and becoming fluent in a second language; living in another culture, which broadens one's mind; travelling, both back to the home country for furloughs and to see grandparents, other family members, and old friends again, but also around Europe on holidays. Besides the yearly one-week Foreign Workers Conference, usually held in France, one summer we spent two weeks in Switzerland using a camper that had been loaned to us by a dear Christian brother. Another summer we spent two weeks in a house of missionary friends in Austria while they went camping with a tent. These were indeed great times!

All three girls attended Capernwray Bible School. Rosa and Renee went to the winter session in southern Germany and the spring session in England, while Lily only attended the winter session in Germany. We'd take them down in September and pick them up for the Christmas holidays, after which we'd take them back again. One time, after having taken one of the girls back at the beginning of January, we were driving home late at night. It was a very lonely road in southern Germany, with the temperature being minus twenty degrees Celsius, when our small diesel car stalled. The fuel filter was frozen, so there we sat, out in the middle of nowhere, with no other car on the road and no house in sight.

156. Again, God's Miraculous Intervention

It was getting cold in the car as we sat there, hoping someone would come by, but it looked like there was nobody else travelling

The God Who is Real

during that cold night. I looked at Marina and said, "Let's pray." Someone may remark, "What good will that do? What can God do in such a situation?" But I prayed and asked the Lord for help. The moment I said "Amen," a thought flashed through my head. I almost shouted at Marina, "Do you have the thermos with you?"

"Yes" she said. "The big one; it's in the back seat."

"What's in it?" I asked.

"Hot water," she answered.

"Hot water? What for?"

"I have some packages of instant soup with me, so I can make you a cup of hot soup."

Ha! Forget the soup. I got out of the car, took the thermos, and poured some of the hot water over the fuel filter. Sure enough, the diesel became fluid again. I waited a bit and turned the key. Praise the Lord, the car started. We began driving, but after about fifteen kilometres it stalled again. I poured more hot water over the filter, and away we went again. I think I did this three or four times before we came upon a lonely service station. The fuel tank was still more than half full, so I explained our problem to the attendant, and he said to put in at least fifteen litres of gasoline and then fill up the rest of the tank with diesel fuel. He said the gasoline would keep the fuel from freezing, and it wouldn't hurt the motor. Off we went, and after many hours of driving through the night with hardly any other cars on the road, we arrived home safely ... very tired, but extremely thankful.

There's no doubt in my mind that the Lord answered our prayer. I had barely finished saying "Amen" when the thought of the thermos flashed through my mind. I didn't even know we had it with us. I know it was the Lord, as I've had more of these experiences. You see, our God is alive and well. *He is real indeed!* What about yours?

157. God's Miraculous Provision

Yes, God is real indeed. We experienced that in so many different ways, small ones and large ones. We experienced that in the peace He gave us, in His wonderful guidance, in the conversion of so many different people, and in the changes we saw in their lives. We also experienced it in our financial situation, which I want to come back to now, as we'd been in Belgium for more than ten years. As you may know, we didn't have a set salary; we lived on gifts from the Lord's people in Canada and a few in the US. We trusted God to move the hearts of people. During those years, the value of the dollar in regards to the Belgian franc, now replaced by the euro, changed quite a bit.

I think it was during our second year that the Canadian dollar was worth approximately seventy-four francs, but it didn't stay there very long. It devalued to fifty francs and then to around forty, where it stayed for quite some time. Before the euro came in, the dollar had gone down to twenty-two francs. Can you imagine? Now comes the amazing thing ... as the value of the dollar went down, our support went up, and more and larger gifts came in. This happened without our supporters realizing what was going on. It was really incredible. But I have to be honest, as the dollar went down, we worried at times as to what would happen to us, yet time and again, more support came in to make up for the loss. This was really amazing! We discovered that there was indeed Someone working behind the scenes and directing all this, praise

God! This has continued throughout the years and right up to the present. I'll tell you more later. It hasn't always been easy, and we've also known difficult times. We've not always been able to buy what we'd like, but He never promised to meet all our wants, He did promise to meet all our needs, and He has been faithful, so we thank and praise Him, as well as the people who allowed themselves to be used by Him to help us.

We have to honestly admit that there are many things about God and His ways that we don't understand, but we know that He is, and that "He is a rewarder of those who diligently seek Him" (Hebrews 11:6). **He is real indeed.** He has proven Himself many a time to us, and I'll tell you more later!

158. Physical Problems

Over the years, I've learned not to go by the things I don't understand, as there are many, but rather to go by what I do understand, and I have learned to understand a lot. I have found that when I walk in the light that I have, more light is given and more is understood.

Previously, I wrote that by 1982, after ten years in Belgium, sixteen churches had started, all praise to God. But as with children, it's one thing to have a baby, but quite another to raise that child to maturity. The same is true with individual Christians and churches. Starting a new church is exciting, but after a while, the difficult work starts: teaching these new believers to get along with each other. That's exciting too, but it's also a lot of work and takes a lot of time, and we had three daughters who were now entering their teenage years. I cut back on some of my activities and started taking Rosa, our oldest, together with a few of her friends, out to go bowling or to music concerts (even a couple in Holland) on Saturday nights, always ending the evening with good old Belgian french fries!

In the fall of 1981, Rosa went to Bodenseehof Capernwray Bible School in southern Germany for the winter semester. There she became ill and should have come home, but she enjoyed the time there so much that she stayed and actually never fully recovered from mononucleosis. In the spring of 1982, she went to Capernwray Bible School in England. In the fall of that year, she went to work at a Christian youth hostel called Ebenezer in Amsterdam for nine months.

On May 18, my birthday, friends took us out for the noon meal and then for a walk in the woods. While there, I suddenly collapsed. They called an ambulance, and I was in the hospital for four days. I was suffering from burnout, which wasn't surprising after having lived in overdrive for some ten years. I had to stop my activities, and we returned to Canada from July until December 1983. In the fall, Rosa went to Prairie Bible Institute in Three Hills, Alberta for a year. She tried going back in 1984, but her health had declined, so she had to return home after a couple of months.

We were back in Belgium by the end of 1983 and continued to witness the work of God's Holy Spirit in the lives of people, as well as the growth of His church. This was exciting indeed!

159. Growth of God's Work Worldwide

From the first of January, 1984, we were back in full swing, and things were still really moving. Over the next ten years, another ten or so churches would be started, and a number of workers would be added. Besides evangelistic Bible studies in homes, there was the work with the churches, and the training of teachers and leaders. Conferences were held, regular baptisms took place, summer camps were in full swing, youth weekends were organized, and a once a month Saturday Bible school was held in two places: Beerse, for the people from that area and from Limburg; and Ghent, for the people from the Antwerp and East and West Flanders regions. Some 175 people took part. We went through most of the Bible, as well as church history and other subjects. Many were blessed and grew in their faith and Christian life.

You know, dear reader, I follow the news every day, as I want to know what's going on in the world, but I get so tired of all the bad news that's brought to us while we don't realize that there are so many good things happening all over the world. When I think back now to those years in Belgium—people saved, lives transformed, broken relationships and marriages restored, and so many other wonderful things—I praise the Lord. Even today in 2017, while there is so much evil in the world, there are so many good things going on. An average of 174.000 people become Christians every day.[3] Never have there been so many Christians in the world as right now. Approximately 3,500 new churches are started every week all over the world.[4] Not only that, but many positive things are done by Christians in needy places, like prisons, hospitals, orphanages, halfway houses, and so on. Many Christian organizations send help to people in Africa, Asia, the Middle East, and other places. Every year, in the US alone, 700 billion dollars are given to Christian causes.[3] More than 78.5 million Bibles are distributed each year.[5] But these things don't make headlines in our newspapers or on TV, yet they are happening, praise God. Oh yes, dear friends, we are on the winning side. Our Lord Jesus Christ will ultimately triumph over all evil, and I'm excited about that. Hallelujah! I hope you're with us! ***God is real all over the world.***

160. God Providing Workers

As already mentioned, because of the rapid growth of the work, it was hard to keep up, so we were very thankful that the Lord raised up other workers to help us. The Luesink's had joined us in 1971, but they returned to Canada in 1974. The Gelling's had come in 1975, the den Boer's in 1976, the Threadcraft's in 1979 (returning to the US in 1983 after a very fruitful ministry in several places), the Symons' in 1981, Dave Dunlap in 1983 (returning to the US in 1989), and the Gifford's in 1984. All of these, except Martin and Lydia Symons, were foreign workers, but now two other Belgian couples came into the work in 1984—Guido and Marianne De Kegel in East Flanders, and Luc and Nicole Vandevorst in Limburg. More would follow in the years to come.

It was in 1977 that I was invited to Guido and Marianne's home to explain the Bible and the gospel. You can read about this in story #133. Guido was a real student, and it wasn't long before he started leading Bible studies, ultimately becoming the best Bible teacher in our churches, and maybe even in all of Flemish Belgium. He also became an elder in the church in Eeklo. He finally felt and obeyed the call of God and took the daring step to leave his good job and start working full-time for the Lord. We were delighted. He's had a great influence on the churches by getting things more organized. During the pioneer phase of a work, things move spontaneously, but after a while, there needs to be some structure and organization. We see this in the New Testament with the growth of the churches. The work of the Lord grew, and the Lord was glorified as His church was being built. In 1983, we went to Canada to visit relatives, friends, our home church, and a number of other churches. It was always so encouraging to meet each other and rejoice together in what the Lord was doing through their prayers and support. By 1984, we were back to the battle in Belgium, and over the next three or four years, all kinds of things happened. There was much to be done, both in evangelism and training of leaders and teachers. The churches were growing … what a joy … but not always without pain, as is usually the case with growth.

161. Rosa's Heartbreaking Illness

The last time we had been in Canada was in 1983. In July 1987, we returned for furlough, which is also called "home assignment." This time it was different, as our oldest daughter, Rosa, was not well at all. She was so weak, she wasn't able to function normally. When she was at Capernwray Bible School in southern Germany, she'd picked up mononucleosis (mono). Because it wasn't treated correctly, it turned into something else. Here are Rosa's own words: "Finally, after eight years of going to doctors in Belgium, Germany, Holland, and Canada, I was diagnosed with M.E." (Myalgic Encephalopathy, not CFS [Chronic Fatigue Syndrome], although the symptoms are similar for some people). About thirty years ago, before Rosa had been diagnosed with M.E., there was much confusion as to what ailed her. It was an extremely difficult time as we sought help, even going to a Christian psychiatrist in the US, but couldn't get any answers. I went to see a doctor in the London, Ontario, area who had the illness himself, but he wasn't able to help us either. We rented an apartment in Elmira and stayed with Rosa, as we didn't feel right leaving her, but it was hard to not be in Belgium where the Lord had called us, so we kept praying and seeking His will.

During the first while that we were back in Canada, our main concern was looking for help for Rosa. At the end of the summer, our other two daughters, Lily and Renee, went back to Belgium to continue their studies and work. They would live in our house, as Lily had her driver's license and could use our car to get around. At the beginning of January 1988, I went back to Belgium for about six weeks, preaching, meeting with workers and church leaders, and speaking at a conference in another European country. The Lord blessed and provided; we were always amazed at His provisions. He knew what we needed and put it upon the hearts of His people to support us. Gifts came in from people we had never met. Really amazing! *Yes, God is real indeed.* We can certainly testify to that. He can be trusted. My trip to Belgium was to be repeated, and that summer, Marina, myself, and Rosa, who was still well enough to travel at that time, went to Europe for something very special.

162. Wedding Bells

Wedding bells were ringing! Yes, our second daughter, Lily, was getting married to a fine Belgian young man, Bart Vanhyfte, on August 6, 1988. In July, Marina, Rosa, and I flew to Belgium to prepare for the wedding, but also to move everything out of our house in Lovendegem, where we had lived for about twelve years. Lily and Renee had been living there the last year and a half, but now they were moving out. Renee was moving into a student house in Ghent, not far from where Lily and Bart had rented a house. We took all our belongings to the church building in Eeklo, which had a large attic where everything could be stored. Some of this was done before the wedding, and the rest after. Renee was a tremendous help, as she really knows how to pack. We're always amazed as to how much she can get into a suitcase or backpack.

The wedding took place on one of the hotter days of that summer in Belgium in an upstairs meeting room above a restaurant. There were many people present, including relatives from Holland. In Belgium, people get married officially at the city hall, after which a church service usually follows. It also happens that people get married "before the law" (as some call it) on Friday and in church on Saturday, after which there is the wedding feast. We had a wonderful service and experienced the Lord's presence and blessing. How thankful we were! There was a reception afterwards. Lily and Bart went on their honeymoon. After they came back, Marina and Rosa returned to Canada, and I stayed to help Renee get settled in. She helped me finish up packing and storing things, after which I flew back to Canada. The separation was difficult for us all.

I left Belgium at the beginning of September with a heavy heart, wondering when we'd be back, if ever. Living in an apartment in Canada with a dear daughter who had an unknown illness, for which there seemed to be no help, I spent many evening hours walking the streets of Elmira, crying to God for help and asking Him what His will was for us. Was this the work of the enemy to keep us out of Belgium? The apostle Paul wrote to the Thessalonians that he wanted to come to them time and again, "but Satan hindered us," (1Thess.2:18) and, strangely enough, God allowed it. It wasn't easy, not for Marina and me, and certainly not for Rosa. But God....!

163. Ministry and Blessing in Canada

I am still firmly convinced that the planting of churches is the best and fastest way to evangelize the world. Therefore, it was a joy to help some established churches grow. The full-time worker at Woodside Bible Chapel in Elmira left, and I was able to assist the elders in visitation and preaching. But what about a new church? Would the Lord use us here to start a new church as we had done in Belgium? It was my constant prayer. I talked to one of the elders at our home church, a dear brother, Abner Frey, and he had a vision for that too. He is now, after a battle with cancer, with the Lord. We talked and prayed together, and I started visiting people in and around Alma, Ontario, not far from Elmira. After some time, a number of people expressed interest in starting up a new work. Towards the end of 1988 and into 1989, we started meeting on Monday evenings in a hall in Alma. I led a study on church doctrines and practices, and after the study we'd discuss what had been taught. It was an exciting time. We moved to a school building and started meeting as a church. Then arrangements were made with the Presbyterian Church to rent their building. This continued for seven and a half years until the school built a major addition, and then the church returned there for three and a half years. In November 1992, land was purchased, and on September 10, 2000, the first Sunday service was held in the new building. Every time I drive through Alma now and pass this building, I thank God for all He has done. There are now about 150–200 people belonging to this church. ***God is real in Canada too.***

164. God's Provision for Rosa

Marina and I prayed and talked a lot about what to do about Rosa's situation. We couldn't find any medical help for Rosa, and because we didn't know what to do or to whom to turn, we decided to go God's way and talk to the elders of our church. We believe that God has instituted authority in the government, in the church, and in the family. Two of the elders and their wives, representing all the elders of our assembly, met with us and told us that they felt very strongly that we were to return to Belgium and continue our God-given ministry there. They offered to take turns caring for Rosa. We prayed together, and then Marina and I, respecting their spiritual place and leadership, felt we should follow their suggestion, trusting God to work things out. It was wonderful of these two couples to be willing to do what they had offered. We felt that as long as we followed God's way, He would guide. And He certainly did; in fact, He had an even better plan. It was decided that we would make a brief trip out West to see Marina' relatives in August and then return to Belgium in September.

A fine retired Christian couple, Burt and Elaine McCollum, lived in Montreal. They had for years been involved in the Lord's work as missionaries with the Union of French Baptist Churches in Canada, and Burt had just resigned from his position. Now they were looking to the Lord as to where He would have them go. Elaine had prayed but received no direction. Then Burt went to his room and sought the Lord, and God put two words on his heart: "Elmira, downtown." He didn't know what to think of that. The next day, a female relative of his who was counselling Rosa called them and asked whether they would be willing to look after a young woman for two weeks while her parents went out West. Burt asked where that would be, and she answered, "In Elmira, downtown!"

165. God's Provision for Buying a House in Belgium

When Marina and I returned from our brief family visit out West, Burt and Elaine told us they felt led by the Lord to stay with Rosa for an indefinite period, as God would lead. They stayed for two and a half years. We were very thankful, knowing that Rosa was in good hands and that the Lord had arranged this! In September, we returned to Belgium. For the time being, we were able to live upstairs in the building owned by the church in Eeklo, where all our possessions had been stored. Two couples from an assembly told us that they would give us an interest free loan if we wanted to buy a house. What an offer! Again, God was looking after us.

We started house hunting, which wasn't easy, but we finally found something in Sint Martens Latem, a very well-to-do town south of Ghent; however, we didn't live in the nice part of the town, but in the lower-class area. Like things are usually done in Belgium, the owner wanted part of the money "in black," as they say. In Canada, we might say, "under the table." This is done so that tax is paid only on the amount on the bill of sale. I told the man that I was a Christian and wouldn't do that. He swore and said "dxxx I'm a Christian too." Ha! He sure proved that. I told him I'd pay him a certain amount extra if we could do everything honestly, and he agreed. We signed and had ourselves a house, but ...

166. Continued Growth of God's Work

Yes, we'd just bought our first house, thanks to the two Belgian couples who gave us interest-free loans. When we sold the house years later, we had enough money to buy the condo we're living in now here in Elmira, Canada, and we still thank the Lord for the love and kindness of these brothers and sisters in Christ who made this possible. We'd bought the house for quite a reasonable price, but it was an old house and needed a lot of renovations. For almost three months, besides holding Bible studies, preaching, and visitation, we worked on the house. Thank God for our co-worker, Hank Gelling, who came from Limburg quite a number of Saturdays, bringing along two or three other men, to help us with the work. In January 1991, we were able to move into it. That same month, on the sixteenth, our first grandchild was born to our second daughter, Lily, and her husband, Bart. Little Emma Vanhyfte was a bundle of joy, and we thanked God for her. And now, in 2017, she is married to an Englishman, and they are together involved in missions.

I'd been holding home Bible studies in the northern part of Ghent, and a number of people had become true born again Christians. Baptisms took place, and these folks joined the Ghent church, which was located in the south of the city. This caused the assembly there to become so large that the building was filled to overflowing. Something needed to be done. To find a larger building was pretty well impossible and not affordable, so a group of believers, many from the north side of Ghent, hived off and started a new church in Mariakerke, a northern suburb of Ghent. This assembly became known as the travelling church, as for different reasons we had to change buildings a number of times. We even met for some time in an old castle in Ghent. In the east of Belgium, the work had continued to grow too, and there were now twelve churches. East Flanders had four, as did West Flanders, and there were four in the Antwerp region. All praise to God! It's wonderful how the Spirit of God moved … amazing! Twenty-four churches in less than twenty years, and in such a difficult West European country. Unbelievable! All we can say is, "Look what the Lord has done!" What a privilege to have been allowed a part in it all. But just as **God is real**, so is the enemy, and we'd experienced his opposition many a time already in different ways. Now, unknown to us, he was attacking again, and we were soon to find that out!

167. Changes

The devil, Satan, is the source of discouragement, confusion, and division. We experienced these things in our own lives and saw it in the lives of other believers and churches. I have written about people becoming Christians and churches being started, much to praise the Lord for, but there were also disappointments and discouragements. Division arose due to differences of opinion about doctrines and church practices. This was now happening in one of our assemblies. Without going into detail, it resulted in a church split, as a group of believers left the church. It was heartbreaking and very painful. There was heart searching, sleepless nights and much prayer, but ultimately the Lord gave victory. After quite some time, the two groups came together, confessed wrong attitudes, and were reunited, praise God. Satan lost that battle!

We continued to work with the new assembly in Mariakerke, and I led Bible studies in some of the other churches. I also continued with evangelistic home Bible studies, especially in the province of West Flanders. There had been a real moving of the Spirit in that part of Belgium with many coming to the Lord; however, things seemed to be changing. We still had full living rooms, but it wasn't quite the same. It seemed that during the period from 1972 to 1992, there was a special moving of God's Spirit, and people seemed to be really interested in the Bible and had many questions. Every week, at times almost every day, some would come to the Lord, but that had really slowed down now. Other evangelical workers noticed it too. Strange. However, when we look at the work of God through the years all over the world, we find that the Spirit seems to work at certain times and in certain areas in special ways. Why that is, I don't know. Has it something to do with God's sovereignty?

Towards the end of 1992, Marina and I returned to Canada for a home assignment and also to check on Rosa, as Burt and Elaine felt that their time was up and they needed to move on. How would the Lord lead this time?

168. Travel and Rest

We had planned to be in Canada for a short time, to be with Rosa and to be in touch with our home church and other supporters, but because Burt and Elaine moved away while Rosa still needed some help, we stayed longer. After Rosa was diagnosed with ME, Elaine helped her get a disability pension. I went back to Belgium on the twenty-third of December and stayed for more than two months, helping believers and churches, and dealing with problems in some places. I also spoke at conferences in France, Germany, and Belarus. There I stayed in Gomel, the second largest city of the country, with friends who worked for World Vision. I was invited to speak to the doctors and nurses of a large hospital. I also had the privilege of speaking to the staff members of the largest women's prison in the country, and Bibles were handed out to all who attended the meeting. The head of the prison was very moved, and I think that she may have accepted the Lord. What struck me most in that country was the absolute poverty—just unbelievable! It made me realize how rich and privileged we are in the West, and how thankful we ought to be!

I flew back to Canada at the end of February, but in April I was back in the Netherlands for my mother's funeral. Because of all the travelling, the meetings, the problems, the emotions, and so on, I was exhausted. I talked to our elders and asked for a six month sabbatical, to which they wholeheartedly agreed. Jesus told his disciples after a very busy time to come apart for a while. Someone has said, "Yes, come apart or else you will come apart." We'd been going pretty steady from 1971 until now, 1993, and it was good to be able to let go of everything for a while.

In December, Marina and I travelled back to Belgium. Rosa received help from the elders for a while, then from the Red Cross, and then from an organization called ILC (Independent Living Centre) for people with disabilities. She has different ladies come in five days a week for two hours to cook, clean, and give help and personal care; they're called "attendants." For the rest of the time, she is on her own and looks after herself. We were happy to be back in the country to which the Lord had called us, but the enemy was not so happy, and 1994 became quite the year, starting with a heart attack!

169. Heart Attack and Hospital Experiences

After a very busy and stressful week in May, we drove to church on a Sunday morning. After having gone only a short distance, I told Marina that I needed some fresh air. I stopped the car, got out, and did some deep breathing. However, this didn't make me feel any better. I also developed a headache, so we turned around and went home and called the doctor, who came to our house. In Belgium, doctors make house calls. He examined me and figured I was hyperventilating. He said to lie down and call him in an hour if things didn't improve. Things did not improve, so he came back, wrote a note, and told us to go to emergency.

When we arrived at the hospital, I gave the doctor's note to a nurse. She read it, grabbed a stretcher, and told me to lie down. I had a smile on my face, and she looked at me and said, "Mr. Haverkamp, you're having a heart attack, and that's no joke."

I think I smiled even more and told her, "Don't worry; if anything happens, I'm ready to go, and I know where I'm going."

She looked at me in surprise and said, "Well, we've never heard those words here before."

I was taken to the intensive care unit and hooked up to all kinds of things. The second night, I woke up in the middle of the night, tore off everything that was attached to me, and got out of bed. The alarm went off right away, and a nurse came running and asked me what I was doing. I said that I was going to take a bath.

"You can't do that," she said.

"Oh yes, I can," I answered. "I'm old enough to make my own decisions." (I didn't realize that I was hallucinating.)

Another nurse came walking in and said, "Mr. Haverkamp, we have the authority here in the hospital."

That word "authority" struck me, and I thought, *Oh yes, the Bible says we are to submit to authority.* "Okay," I said, turning around and getting into bed again. The next morning, I remembered everything and apologized to the nurses, but they laughed and told me that it happens quite often. It's the medication that does it, so we all had a good laugh together.

Thank God that Marina had been able to get her Belgian driver's license when we'd returned from Canada and for a brief period were living in the church building in Eeklo. Right across the road was the driving school, so she'd gone there and had done both her written as well as her road test and passed. A friend who was an instructor had told me that Marina would never make it because of her age and her language problems, as the questions are very tricky. The fact that she made it testifies that the Lord helped her through this. What a blessing now, as she could get around and also come and visit me in the hospital.

170. God's Work Prospers in Spite of Second Heart Attack and Back Operation

My cardiologist had told me I'd lost twenty per cent of my heart functioning and needed to rest a lot and take it easy. It was very difficult for me to have to cancel Bible studies and speaking engagements. My dear wife sure looked after me well. One afternoon I was pulling some weeds from our lawn and, while bent over, I turned a bit and heard a pop in my lower back. As I straightened out it started hurting, but it wasn't too bad. I could sit and bear it while we had company from Antwerp. When I got up the next morning and was putting on a sock, however, something popped again, and this time it really hurt. When I stood up, I couldn't get my left foot down to the floor. It was really bad. Marina phoned the doctor, who came and gave me a needle for the pain. He looked at me and said, "I've never seen anyone so white." For a whole week I lay in bed with my legs high up on pillows, but it didn't improve. The doctor called an ambulance, which took me to the hospital. I was there for a week while they did some tests and came to the conclusion that I had a herniated disc in my lower back and needed surgery. The day after the operation, in the evening, an alarm sounded. The nurse quickly turned the end of my bed up so that my head was lowered and my feet raised. Blood was taken, and soon the news came that I'd suffered a second heart attack. So back to intensive care. After about ten days I was allowed to go home, but had to stay in bed. To keep the story short, altogether I was flat on my back for fifty-five days. "God never promised us an easy journey, but He has promised us His peace."

While I was laid up, the work of the Lord continued. People were still being saved and added to the churches; however, things were changing. The first twenty or so years had been the pioneer's phase when many came to the Lord and many churches were started, but now we entered into the stabilizing phase. More structure was needed; leaders had to be trained, and believers needed to grow. As exciting as the conversion of many people had been, this phase, seeing people mature and become active in Sunday school work, camp activities, leadership in the church and other activities, was just as rewarding. Jesus was building His church in Belgium, step by step, and at that point, without me. Wonderful!

171. More New Workers but also Sadness

The Lord added several new workers to our team. In 1990, Rosario and Anita Anastasi became very active in Limburg. In 1991, Eric and Lut Rutten came from Limburg to help in West Flanders, doing a great work of teaching Bible studies, preaching, and counselling. Eric Schrapen and his wife joined us in 1992 for five years, being active in evangelism and teaching, mainly in Limburg. More would follow later. We were very thankful for all these, especially after my two heart attacks and back operation, as I noticed that I didn't have the same energy as before. It took quite some time to get some strength back.

In the fall of 1994, a small group of believers left the assembly in the south of Ghent over doctrinal differences. It was very painful, as those folks were very dear to us. But these things happen. Even two great apostles, Paul and Barnabas, differed on something and went their separate ways. It was so good to have

Pete and Joanna Gifford working with us in Ghent. They were mainly involved in the Ghentbrugge assembly, while Marina and I helped in the Mariakerke church. Pete was very active in youth work, youth weekends, and camp work. Marina was also involved for many years in camp work, both in the children's camps as well as the youth camps. Of course, her accordion always went along. Not only did she often play for the singing, but some of the children and youth used to enjoy playing with it too.

In 1996, we went back to Canada for a home assignment from April until July. It was wonderful to see Rosa again after almost three years, and to spend time with our home church and other supporting churches and friends. It was always so good to be able to tell them what the Lord was doing in Belgium through their prayers and financial help. It was so encouraging for them!

172. More about God's Provisions

One of the blessings we experienced was the wonderful way in which the Lord provided for His children through His children. God had called us to preach the unsearchable riches of Christ and to plant churches. According to the Bible, a church is not a building, but a group (assembly) of believers; however, when such a group becomes too large, a building is needed. There were two assemblies in Ghent: one in the south end, in Ghentbrugge, and one in the north, in Mariakerke. The one in Mariakerke had to change buildings a number of times, and now they had to again move out of their building. There was no other place to go, so it was decided that for the time being, the two churches would meet together on Sunday morning. This wasn't really a satisfactory solution, so after much prayer and discussion, it was decided to have the two churches buy a building together, as one alone couldn't afford that. We needed to know how everyone felt about this and how much money we could count on, so we drew up a letter to give to all the believers as well as to some in other assemblies, asking if they could give a onetime gift and/or an interest free loan. The results were amazing. Enough money was promised for us to start looking for a suitable building to buy. It was clear that the Lord was in this, and we praised Him. I can't go into all the details, but we did find a building, which was a house with a large hall behind it that used to be a print shop. The deal was made, and now the renovations began. But there was one problem. We were pretty well out of money, so now what? We would soon find out that the Lord had a couple of surprises for us!

173. God's Wonderful Surprises

The first surprise was four men coming from the UK organization Brass Tacks, an organization with the following mission: "Our mission is to relieve missionaries and full-time Christian workers of their maintenance, mechanical, and building work. We build new or renovate existing buildings." The four men helped us for two weeks free of charge. They did a tremendous amount of work and really knew what they were doing. I don't know how we ever could have gotten things done without them; it was a real provision from the Lord.

The second surprise was almost unbelievable. These men encouraged me to write to another Christian organization in the UK whose goal was to provide financial support. Seeing that I had spoken in several churches and at a couple conferences in the UK, I may have been no stranger to them. I wrote them and told them very honestly what was going on and how we'd come to the end of our finances. Within a week or so, I received a very, very large cheque—enough to cover pretty well all of the renovations. The Christians in Ghent were so surprised and amazed that people in England would send money to people whom they had never met. It was indeed the Lord providing for His children through His children. It was wonderful, but that's how the body of Christ, the family of God, works.

174. The Opening of the Building in Ghent

Marina and I were planning a trip to Canada, as it had already been three years since our last visit. We'd be leaving in September and returning towards the end of the year or the beginning of the next year. While in Canada for several months, we were able to stay in the home of Allan and Helena Hoffman, who were going out of the country on a mission trip. They even let us use their car. We thanked God for them and for another one of His provisions. We had a precious time with Rosa and also with our home church and other people and churches that supported us. I was speaking in a different assembly every Sunday, and at some weeknight meetings.

We flew back to Belgium at the beginning of January and were glad to be able to continue our ministry there. The new building in Ghent wasn't finished yet, as there were many little things to be done. After painting the whole place, we were able to start using it, which was a real joy. We had also planned an official opening to which we could invite the neighbours and other folks. We talked about inviting the mayor of Ghent, but someone laughed and said that he would never come, as he was a real socialist and never entered church buildings, not even when the King would visit Ghent. However, one of our church members, a doctor, was also a city councillor, talked to the mayor, who accepted the invitation. As the building was filling up with Christians and non-Christians, we wondered whether or not he would keep his word. Sure enough, there he came, with his wife! What an unbelievable surprise! Who would have ever thought that! We had a wonderful meeting with singing and speeches. Even the mayor spoke, after which I spoke, or rather preached. I doubt whether this man had ever heard the gospel, but he sure did that afternoon, as I didn't beat around the bush. As I was speaking, I wondered what his response would be. At a reception after the meeting, the mayor came to me and thanked me for my words. He was very positive. Incredible! His wife was very enthusiastic and thanked me several times, telling me how much she'd enjoyed everything, especially my speech. I asked her whether she had a Bible, which she didn't, so she went home with one. She told me that a few times while ironing clothes, she'd watched the Evangelical Broadcast from Holland. The seed has been sown; eternity will reveal what has happened to it. In the entrance hall a plaque is on the wall with the words: *"On May 5, 2000, this building of the Evangelical Christian Church was officially opened by Mr. Frank Beke, Mayor of the city of Ghent."* We praised God for this. And so rejoicing in the Lord, we went on with His work.

175. A Shocking Experience in Canada

When one is busy and has much to do, time just flies, so two years went by in no time. In August 2002, we returned to Canada for our fortieth wedding anniversary. This time we had Lily and her husband with us, plus their three daughters. This was the girls' first time in Canada. Renee was living in Israel at the time and wasn't able to come. Rosa, who was still fairly well at that time, together with Carol, Marina's youngest sister, who lived in Chatham, Ontario, planned the whole party. It was a wonderful time in every way, and we all thanked God for His blessings.

While Lily, Bart, and the three girls returned to Belgium, Marina and I stayed to speak in different assemblies in Ontario and then drive west, holding meetings along the way in Manitoba, Saskatchewan, and Alberta, while also visiting family. The meetings and visits were all lined up, and we were going to be starting out shortly after September 15, our wedding date. On that day, we drove to a church in Ethel, about forty-five minutes from us. I was to speak there that morning. We started with the Lord's Supper, and different people took part. Then the bread and cup were shared to remember the Lord Jesus. After that, the collection plate was passed around to receive gifts of thanksgiving. Marina looked at me and saw that my head was down, my eyes were closed, and my face was as white as a sheet. When she touched my arm, it felt as cold as ice. Thinking I'd suffered another heart attack, she jumped up and cried out, "My husband is dead!"

176. A Change of Plans

No, I wasn't dead. After a few moments, I opened my eyes, lifted my head, and saw a lot of people standing around me. I asked, "Was I away for a bit?" They nodded their heads. I felt very weak and was trembling. Someone brought a glass of water, and I slowly got to my feet, shaking quite a bit. Most of the people had gone downstairs for coffee, and shortly I went down too, with someone helping me. I realized that I wasn't up to preaching, and the folks told me to go to the hospital and get checked. I was still feeling pretty miserable, so Marina and I drove to the hospital in Listowel, where a doctor examined me, concluding that it had not been a heart attack. I had fainted, likely due to over-tiredness and the warm weather. The last six weeks had been very busy.

The next day, I still felt very weak and tired, and we realized that it wasn't possible to make the long trip out West now. We phoned and emailed all our contacts, and new dates were set. We were able to stay in a house in Gorrie, Ontario, that belonged to missionaries who were on the mission field. It was a very quiet place, and we were able to get rested up. After I regained my strength, we started out for the West. We had a good trip, wonderful meetings, and great times with family and friends. We returned to Elmira, and after spending time with Rosa, we flew back to Belgium.

We continued to help the assembly in Mariakerke, Ghent, while I also led Bible studies and preached in other churches. Time was spent meeting with men who were or would become elders in the churches. Marina was on the phone a lot, encouraging people, and she also spent much time writing cards and letters. Towards the end of August 2004, we drove to France to attend the yearly Foreign Workers Conference. We arrived at the large hotel where the conference was held, and the organizers showed us a quiet room at the end of the hallway—at least, they thought it was quiet! We arrived quite late and went straight to bed, but then …

177. Marina in Trouble

Suddenly, we heard a tremendous noise from below us—musical instruments, loud singing, and shouting. What we didn't know, and I don't think the organizer knew either, was that there was another floor below us with a ballroom. The noise was so overwhelming that I left our room to see what was going on and discovered that a group of handicapped young people were there to make music, dance, and have a ball. The rock and roll music was very loud, and it came right up into our room. I'll let Marina tell you in her own words how she felt: "It started with the feeling of a trains wheels going through my body, starting at the stomach, through the heart, and ending up in my throat. I tried to sing and pray, but it kept on and on. We read in the Bible, 'The troubles of my heart are enlarged, O Lord, bring me out of my distress.' This was my inner cry. Richard prayed with me, and finally the music and noise stopped and there was blessed quietness."

I went looking in the hallway for some help, but it was late and everyone was asleep; besides, we didn't know where "our" people were, as there were other guests in the hotel too. Since I don't speak French, I didn't want to talk to someone at the desk. It took quite some time for Marina's heart to be at ease and beat normally again. We did sleep for some hours, but were up early and decided to go home, as we felt the busyness of the meetings, meals, and discussions would be too much for Marina, who needed quietness.

We arrived home and called our cardiologist for an appointment. He had Marina do a stress test and said that everything seemed to be alright, but Marina knew it wasn't.

A week or so later, Marina was not feeling well again, so we returned to the cardiologist, who put a monitor on her for a week. The day after we returned it, he called and asked me to come and see him as soon as possible. In his office, he told me that they had found something irregular and gave me some special medication for Marina. He also told me that if anything abnormal were to happen to go to emergency immediately. Saturday night at 11:45, Marina felt miserable again, so I took her blood pressure, which was 183/33 (normal = 120/80), and her pulse, which was twenty-two (normal = seventy)!

178. God Spared Marina, and Future Plans

Without hesitation we got into the car and drove to the hospital. I told the nurses about her blood pressure and heart rate. They immediately took her to the intensive care unit, where they hooked her up to a monitor, gave her intravenous drugs, and kept checking her. A nurse told me to go home and get some rest. "Your wife is in good hands," she said.

The next day was Sunday, so on my way to church to preach I saw Marina. She told me that the night before an alarm had sounded and a nurse came running over. Marina saw that her heart beat on the monitor was just a little flicker. The nurse said she was going to get a doctor. Marina told her she was fine, and in God's hands and not worried, as she was not afraid to die. She then passed out and woke up Sunday morning feeling better. She said she had no idea what they had done with her during the night, but she was not in heaven, but still in the intensive care unit. At church, I asked the Christians to pray for her. The next day, a pacemaker was put in, and soon she was much better. It had been a close call; I almost lost her, but the Lord had kept her, and we praised Him.

We went back to our activities, but we both felt that we didn't have the same energy as before, so we started wondering and praying about our future. We felt the time might come when we may have to return to Canada, as we didn't think it right for our home church and others who were supporting us to continue if we weren't able to do what we used to do. It would be better for our financial support to go to new and younger missionaries. We didn't know what the future held, so we wondered about selling our house and renting another, so that if we had to leave suddenly, we wouldn't have the hassle of getting rid of our house.

During the summer of 2005, on a Friday afternoon, we had a realtor come to discuss the matter with us. He was willing to sell our house, and we told him the amount we wanted for it. He smiled and told us that we would never get that, since it was such an old house. He promised to be back on Monday morning to take pictures to put on his website, but Monday morning came and he did not show up. Instead, a lady rang our doorbell. We had no idea that several miracles were about to happen.

179. Miracles

Marina opened the door and greeted the lady standing there, who said that she'd heard from our neighbour that our house may be up for sale. Marina was quite surprised and explained that I wasn't home, and asked her to come back later. The lady said she would come back with her husband, as they were interested in our house. Later that day they returned. He was the police commissioner for southern Ghent. Their unmarried daughter was also with the police force, and they were looking to buy a house for her. We showed them the whole house, garage, and yard, and they said they were definitely interested and could come back the next morning to meet our realtor. After they left, I phoned him and told him that we had some folks who were interested in our house. When I told him their name, he laughed and said not to expect much, as he had shown them a number of houses already, and every time they were interested, but then changed their minds.

The next morning the couple returned, as did the realtor. He went through the whole house with them, left them upstairs, came down to us, and asked us again how much we wanted for the house. I told him that he already knew that and that we were sticking to that price. He frowned and went back upstairs. A little later, the three of them came down with smiles on their faces. Yes, they wanted the house and agreed to the price. Unbelievable! Not only that, but I had a list of some twenty-three things that needed to be done to the house before we thought we could sell it. The policeman told us not to do anything, as they would fix up the house the way they wanted it. He had also studied to be an architect and loved to fix up old buildings. What a relief, as I was quite worried about all the work that needed to be done and how I would get it all done. Talk about a miracle! The realtor was so impressed that he and his wife took us out for a very expensive dinner, and we had a great opportunity to witness to them. ***Oh yes, God is so real!***

180. Amazing Intervention of God

Miracle number two: together with the buyers, we went to a lawyer to get all the legal paperwork done. She was a very nice and friendly lady who had a young man, her secretary, present also. She had a list of fourteen things that needed to be looked into and checked. I was asked about mortgages, and I answered that we didn't have any. She looked surprised and asked how we were able to buy the house. When I told her what had happened, she was absolutely amazed!

"Well," she said, "I've never heard of anything like that."

I'd told her that we were part of an evangelical church, or community, and that two couples had given us interest-free loans so that we could buy the house. Everything had been paid back by now, and I offered to give her the names and addresses of these couples so she could check to see if this was true. She shook her head and told her secretary that he didn't need to do that, because she believed and trusted us. Maybe reading our wedding booklet had touched her heart. We had to prove that we were married, and unlike in Belgium where people have an official marriage booklet, in Canada, many people are married in a church by a minister who has a license and can sign the marriage certificate. We had this certificate inside a booklet with the wedding vows and order of service. One of Marina's sisters, who has a beautiful voice, sang a song based on the words in Ruth 1: "Wherever you go, I will go."

The lawyer smiled when she saw that and told us that was sung at her wedding also. Interesting!

She then told us that it would take three months to check everything, after which the deal would be official. I told her that we were going to Canada on September 27 for a three-month visit, and we would very much like to have things settled before then. It was about the middle of August at that point, so it seemed almost impossible to have things finished by that date. She looked at us, smiled, and told us that she would give us priority and that she was quite sure we would have our money before we left. And we did. A couple of days before leaving for Canada, everything was completed. Unbelievable! **Yes, God is real indeed.**

There was something else we had worried about. In Belgium, as in some other countries, when deals are done, often people will do things under the table so they don't have to pay as much tax. When we bought this house, the owner wanted to do part of it under the table, but I refused and instead gave him extra money. Now we were the ones selling. What if the buyer insisted on doing that too? Well, that problem never came up, as the buyer was a chief of police. I imagine he couldn't risk doing something unlawful. Ha! We rejoiced and thanked the Lord. But now we had approximately six weeks to find another house. To us, that seemed almost impossible, but God ...

181. Divine Guidance and Provision

We were very thankful that our house sold overnight, but we weren't looking forward to driving all over the place to look for a house to rent and fix up, and then move again in six weeks. As I drove to the store one morning, I came to the street where I was to turn left, but "something" inside me said, "Turn right." I hesitated for a moment, but then turned right. Just a little way down the road, again "something" said, "Turn left." I did, and after approximately 150 metres, I saw a nice bungalow with a sign out front: "For Rent." I took the phone number, went to the store, and then drove home and told Marina about this. I asked her whether she would like to go and see this house. She agreed, and we drove over. I rang the doorbell, and a lady opened the door. I asked her about the house, which she was renting. We looked it over, and it was just right. Marina said right away, "That's for us!" That morning, we had read Psalm 25:12, which says, "Who is the man that fears the Lord? Him shall He teach in the way He chooses."

There were several suitcases standing in the hallway, and the lady told us that she was going on holidays to Spain the next day. "You caught me just in time," she said. We talked things over and were able to buy her curtains, her dishwasher, and several other things. We went home, phoned the owners, had a meeting with them that evening, and rented the house. Unbelievable! The rent was a bit high, but the wonderful thing was that we didn't have to do any fixing up at all—no painting, no wallpapering, no new rugs to put in. We could move right in without spending a cent. This was the first time that we were able to do that; all other times, we had to spend a lot of money and a lot of time fixing up a house. Now everything was just perfect. What a relief and what a provision from the Lord! Before the move, we had to dispose of a lot of things we didn't need that had been collected over the years. Thank God for Robert, a dear Christian brother, who helped me much of the time. I don't know what I would have done without him. Finally, shortly before leaving for Canada, we moved into our "dream house" provided by the Lord. What a joy!

182. Family Reunion in Canada

It had been about three years since our last visit to Canada, and now after several months of visiting family and friends there and preaching approximately thirty times, we returned to Belgium. But during the summer of 2006, we went back to Canada with our whole family, as there was going to be a Funk (Marina's) family reunion. It had been many years since the last one, and our granddaughters had never met their Canadian relatives.

The Lord was so good to us and provided for us. We flew to Calgary, Alberta, where one of Marina's brothers had rented two cars for us. We drove to the home of another of Marina's brothers, who had a farm just outside of Three Hills, Alberta. Our granddaughters were so impressed with the outstretched landscape and the long roads. While driving on one of these, one of the girls said, "Is this road never going to end?" Imagine their surprise when a day or so later we drove from the farm onto the highway, turned left, and stayed on that road for about 500 kilometres through part of Alberta and Saskatchewan, and then turned right into Pike Lake Provincial Park, where the reunion was being held. It was a wonderful weekend indeed, with at least 110 family members present. Marina comes from a family of eleven. Our children and grandchildren flew back to Belgium, while Marina and I took a plane to Toronto to spend some time with Rosa, who, because of her illness, hadn't been able to be at the reunion.

The next three years in Belgium were spent preaching, teaching, visiting, and meeting with church leaders, while Marina continued encouraging women through visitation and over the phone. At the same time, we were getting more and more tired, and I was starting to find it difficult to deal with some of the problems. We began to wonder about our future. There were some twenty-four churches now and quite a number of workers. Should we continue in Belgium, even though we weren't able to be as active as before? Was it right for our home church and others to keep supporting us financially? Should that support not go to younger workers?

In 2008, we made a trip to Canada to see how the Lord would lead.

183. Return to Canada?

There were several reasons why we were thinking of returning to Canada. Already mentioned was our physical condition; we were really tired. I guess that was the result of years living in overdrive. Another one was the fact that we didn't feel right about being fully financially supported when we weren't able to be as active as before. On top of that, our health insurance was running out. In Marina's case, it already had. We were with a company in Canada that insured missionaries, but only up to the age of seventy. Then they were expected to return to Canada and be covered by government insurance. Our church graciously covered the monthly premiums. Staying in Belgium would mean getting private insurance, which is very costly. And then, of course, there was our daughter, Rosa, who, because of her debilitating illness, had been without us, her sisters, and her nieces and nephews for many years. We felt we should be near her now.

We prayed a lot about this and talked to the elders of our church. They were in agreement with our returning to Canada and were ready to give us a letter of commendation for full-time work in Canada. We also asked the advice of good friends, who were in accord with our move back. Since Marina was no longer covered by health insurance and was having heart problems, we felt we should go ahead and plan our return. We were at perfect peace about all of this, so we started looking for a place to live. After driving all around Elmira, I found a house on a quiet street that was up for sale. The elderly lady who owned the house showed me around but then changed her mind. It was sort of disappointing, but we left it in the Lord's hands and returned to Belgium. In April 2009, we received a call from good friends in Elmira telling us that there was a condo for sale in a seniors' building. Our friends took pictures of the condo and emailed them to us. We thought they looked great and were quite excited. We really prayed about it and felt perfect peace. After more discussion with our friends there, a few days later I was on a plane to Toronto.

184. Buying a Condo in Canada and Saying Farewell to Folks in Belgium

Why the hurry? Because there were others interested in this condo. Our friends had asked the person responsible to wait and give me a chance to see it. I arrived in Toronto, was picked up, and together with our friends went to see the place. I walked through it, took a good look at it, and knew it was for us. The financial side had to be arranged, which took time, but then on the fourth day, I flew back to Belgium ... owning a condo in Elmira. Praise the Lord! Marina and I decided not to move until the fall, as I had a lot of speaking engagements lined up and we had to get rid of a lot of things. We had arrived in Belgium in December 1971 and were leaving in October 2009, so after thirty-eight years, there was a lot to leave there. I just want to mention this yet, we bought the condo in April and moved at the end of October, but from April until October, another missionary couple, Les and Sharon Frey, who were working in Spain, were on furlough and were able to make use of our condo. It came together so well, praise God!

Quite a number of our churches in Belgium organized farewell parties for us, either alone or with a couple of others, and there was a final farewell with all the churches together before we left. These meetings were wonderful but also painful, as we were saying goodbye to many spiritual children whom we dearly loved. Many were in tears, as we were at times. I had quite a library, with hundreds and hundreds of books, and since I couldn't take all of them with me to Canada, I took a number of boxes with books along to the meetings, put them out on tables, and told the people they could take them and donate whatever they wanted.

Slowly we were getting rid of things, selling some of our furniture and giving away some. Our daughters helped us pack boxes and boxes full with dishes, clothes, and many other things. We had all kinds and sizes of boxes. A friend had an export company and arranged the moving of our possessions by boat to Canada. We agreed to meet a certain day, bring all our boxes, and pack them into eight large and strong cartons which our friend would bring. But could we get everything into those?

185. Packing, Shipping, and Leaving

The day came when everything was ready to be packed and shipped, so we took all our boxes, small ones and big ones, to our friend's warehouse, where we started packing them into his eight cartons. We filled carton after carton until we came to the last one, and now comes the surprise. The last carton was almost full; we had only one box left—the one with Marina's accordion, and believe me or not, the accordion went in perfectly. There wasn't any room left ... really! Unbelievable! No one could have planned it better! Did we get help from above? I am sure!

Finally, the day before we were to leave, which was Thursday, October 15, 2009, arrived. We were taking the train from Ghent at 7:10 a.m., as going to the airport by car at that hour in the morning is very risky because of traffic jams. Our children, Lily, her husband Bart, and Renee went along, as did our youngest grandchild, Hanne. They wanted to see us off at the airport. Bart and Lily were going to pick us up in the morning and drive us to the train station, while Renee went straight from her house. And so came the last night in that wonderful house. We didn't have to clean it, as our daughters were going to do that after we left.

To be sure we had a good sleep, Marina and I took a light sleeping pill and went to bed. It was pitch dark in our bedroom, as there were blinds over the windows. We must have been sound asleep when all at once I heard the doorbell ring. I woke up and wondered who in the world would be there at this time of the night. When I opened the door, I saw Bart and Lily with Hanne.

"Dad, it's 6:45 a.m. We have to leave right now."

Marina and I had slept in and not heard the alarm. We've never gotten dressed so fast. We just left everything and jumped into the car. In my haste, I forgot my wallet. Thinking we would never make it to the station in time, Lily phoned Renee to tell her to ask the station manager to hold the train until we arrived. Of course, they never do that. But we were "lucky." There were so many people going on the train that day that they had to add two carriages. That took a little time ... enough for us to get there and on the train! Praise the Lord! Then we started laughing, and we still laugh when we think of that.

186. Arriving and Settling Down in Canada

From the train, onto the plane, and off to Canada. Leaving our family behind was hard on all of us, but knowing we were all in the will of the Lord and in the hands of our God made a difference. We arrived in Canada on Thursday, October 15, 2009. For the first two weeks, we stayed with friends while our condo was being painted and new rugs were put in. I had rented a car to shop around for one. Because of my back problems, I needed one that sits quite high. New ones were too expensive, and the right second-hand one was hard to find. I don't know how many car dealers I visited, but I was sure getting tired. Saturday came and I drove to Guelph. To make the story short, within half an hour I had found the right car for the right price, $500 less than what I received for our car sold in Belgium ... wonderful! Rosa told me later that she had asked the Lord to "drop a car into my lap." I believe He did, praise Him!

We moved into our condo, and a couple of weeks later our boxes from Belgium arrived. While the fridge, couch, bed, and TV were bought new, the rest of the furniture was all second-hand.

Richard Haverkamp

We had a great time visiting Salvation Army stores in Kitchener/Waterloo, where we were able to pick up some really good things for a cheap price.

We've been here now for almost eight years; it's unbelievable how fast time goes. It was great to be able to make a 9,000 kilometre trip out West to visit Marina's family and also friends and churches that had been supporting us from time to time. Except for the last year and a half, I preached every Sunday and also at some weeknight meetings. Marina spends much of her time phoning and writing cards to folks in Belgium. In 2015, I had a serious breakdown and had to stop all activity, but slowly I am improving and preaching again. Marina had colon cancer surgery in December 2015, but is now completely clean. ***God's peace was so real.*** She also received a new pacemaker just in time. I had prostate surgery in May, which went well. We don't have the strength that we used to have, and that is frustrating at times, but we have to accept our limitations. This is life. The Lord continues to provide for us, at times in amazing ways, for which we praise Him.

The God Who is Real

The car which the Lord "dropped in my lap"
in answer to my daughter's prayer.

187. The End. YES, God Is Real Indeed

Yes, this is the end. I started writing in February 2013, and I began with this: "My wife and I were just married fifty years (in September 2012), and we have been serving the Lord together for all those years. We would like to share some of our experiences and answers to prayer with the purpose of showing that **God is really real!**"

So how did we experience that God is really real? We have found it in His very real guidance, showing us when and where to

Richard Haverkamp

move. We also found it in the way He's provided for us all these years, so often in miraculous ways. We have felt His presence and peace. As the Word was preached, we saw Him working in the hearts and lives of people, many becoming born again Christians and many lives and marriages being changed ... just wonderful! In Bible studies, prayer meetings, church meetings, and conferences all over Europe, we have experienced the powerful working of His Spirit, and we have been filled with the joy of the Lord. ***Oh yes, God is real indeed!***

We'd like to thank the Christians in Belgium for the joy they have brought to our hearts. How we miss them! We had expected to make a trip to Belgium by now, but due to poor health, this has not been possible. But we keep in touch by phone, Facebook, and email. We also want to take the opportunity to thank the believers of our home church for all the years they have stood with us, and we also thank other churches and Christians who have prayed for us and supported us financially. God has done great things in Belgium and Europe, and this has been because of the teamwork of those going and others staying and supporting.

We want to make mention that in all of our comings and goings, and moving from place to place as God led us, our daughters, Rosa, Lily, and Renee were part of our work, helping in new Sunday schools, Bible clubs, camps, and other activities. We are so thankful that all three know the Lord. Rosa lives across the road from us in her own apartment. Lily and Bart live in Belgium. Their two oldest daughters are both married to Englishmen, and the second daughter, Kaat, had her first baby on October 1, 2016. The youngest daughter, Hanne, is living in England also and continues her theological studies. Our youngest daughter, Renee, lives here in Elmira. The last time we were all together as a family was our fiftieth wedding anniversary in 2012.

And now I must close. We could have written so much, much more, but …! I plan to continue writing stories and articles on Facebook and on our Blog, www.richardandmarina.net. When you go there and click on "Follow," you will get my next article in your email inbox.

A last thank you to all the readers who read this story on Facebook or on our blog and who sent us meaningful comments. Also, thank you to the many who suggested putting this in book form. May God bless you all.

This then is our story and how we experienced the reality of the living God—**His presence, His guidance, His provisions, His protection, His faithfulness, and His blessings!** We can unequivocally say, *God is real indeed.*

And now, dear reader, how about you, are you experiencing that God is real? Have you acknowledged your sinful condition and received God's gift, the Lord Jesus Christ, into your heart? Then you too will experience that *He is real indeed.*

Have you also surrendered your life completely to Him? I would challenge you to do so on a daily basis as you walk with God and you will discover how God is going to work in and through you.

May the true God, who is so real, bless and guide you.

Richard and Marina.

If you have any questions or comments, feel free to email us at: rhaverkamp7@gmail.com

End notes

1. http://www.warrenapologeticscenter.org/blog/there-will-be-no-singing.html. (Accessed June 12, 2017)
2. "Ypres in War and Peace."Pirkin Guides Ltd, latest reprint 1997. Printed in Great Britain. (Accessed June 12, 2017
3. https://www.thoughtco.com/christianity-statistics-700533. (Accessed June 12, 2017)
4. https://www.thoughtco.com/christianity-statistics-700533. (Accessed June 12, 2017)
5. https://static1.squarespace.com/static/4f661fde24ac1097e013deea/t/550f7d77e4b0907feba099b0/1427078519637/StatusGlobalChristianity2015_CSGC_IBMR.pdf (Accessed June 12, 2017)
6. Available from http://www.thetravelingteam.org/articles/growth-of-the-church. (Accessed June 12, 2017)

The God Who is Real

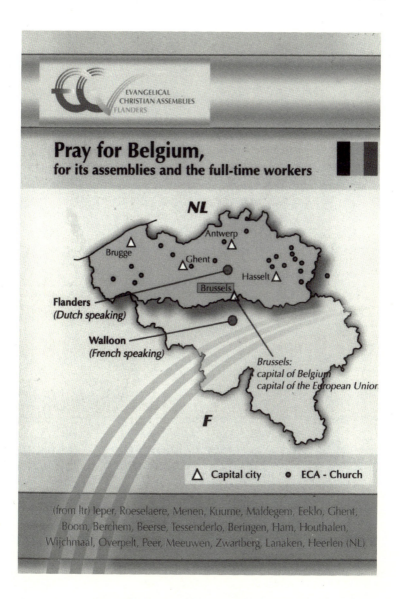

Map of Belgium with most of the churches.

Printed in Canada